INTRODUCING
ISSUES WITH
OPPOSING
VIEWPOINTS®

Military
Draft

INTRODUCING
ISSUES WITH
OPPOSING
VIEWPOINTS®

Military
Draft

Other books in the Introducing Issues
with Opposing Viewpoints series:

INTRODUCING
ISSUES WITH
OPPOSING
VIEWPOINTS®

Military Draft

George Milite, *Book Editor*

Christine Nasso, *Publisher*
Elizabeth Des Chenes, *Managing Editor*

GREENHAVEN PRESS
An imprint of Thomson Gale, a part of The Thomson Corporation

THOMSON

GALE

Detroit • New York • San Francisco • New Haven, Conn. • Waterville, Maine • London

For more information, contact
Greenhaven Press
27500 Drake Rd.
Farmington Hills, MI 48331-3535
Or you can visit our Internet site at http://www.gale.com

LIBRARY OF CONGRESS CATALOGING-IN-PUBLICATION DATA

Military draft / George Milite, book editor.
   p. cm. — (Introducing issues with opposing viewpoints)
    Includes bibliographical references and index.
    ISBN-13: 978-0-7377-3601-4 (hardcover : alk. paper)
    ISBN-10: 0-7377-3601-1 (hardcover : alk. paper)
  1. Military service, Voluntary—United States—Juvenile literature. 2. Draft—United States—Juvenile literature.
   UB323.M535 2007
   355.2'23630973—dc22

                              2006027922

Contents

Foreword

Indulging in a wide spectrum of ideas, beliefs, and perspectives is a critical cornerstone of democracy. After all, it is often debates over differences of opinion, such as whether to legalize abortion, how to treat prisoners, or when to enact the death penalty, that shape our society and drive it forward. Such diversity of thought is frequently regarded as the hallmark of a healthy and civilized culture. As the Reverend Clifford Schutjer of the First Congregational Church in Mansfield, Ohio, declared in a 2001 sermon, "Surrounding oneself with only like-minded people, restricting what we listen to or read only to what we find agreeable is irresponsible. Refusing to entertain doubts once we make up our minds is a subtle but deadly form of arrogance." With this advice in mind, Introducing Issues with Opposing Viewpoints books aim to open readers' minds to the critically divergent views that comprise our world's most important debates.

Introducing Issues with Opposing Viewpoints simplifies for students the enormous and often overwhelming mass of material now available via print and electronic media. Collected in every volume is an array of opinions that captures the essence of a particular controversy or topic. Introducing Issues with Opposing Viewpoints books embody the spirit of nineteenth-century journalist Charles A. Dana's axiom: "Fight for your opinions, but do not believe that they contain the whole truth, or the only truth." Absorbing such contrasting opinions teaches students to analyze the strength of an argument and compare it to its opposition. From this process readers can inform and strengthen their own opinions, or be exposed to new information that will change their minds. Introducing Issues with Opposing Viewpoints is a mosaic of different voices. The authors are statesmen, pundits, academics, journalists, corporations, and ordinary people who have felt compelled to share their experiences and ideas in a public forum. Their words have been collected from newspapers, journals, books, speeches, interviews, and the Internet, the fastest growing body of opinionated material in the world.

Introducing Issues with Opposing Viewpoints shares many of the well-known features of its critically acclaimed parent series, Opposing Viewpoints. The articles are presented in a pro/con format, allowing readers to absorb divergent perspectives side by side. Active reading questions preface each viewpoint, requiring the student to approach the material thoughtfully and carefully. Useful charts, graphs, and cartoons supplement each article. A thorough introduction provides readers with crucial background on an issue. An annotated bibliography points the reader toward articles, books, and Web sites that contain additional information on the topic. An appendix of organizations to contact contains a wide variety of charities, nonprofit organizations, political groups, and private enterprises that each hold a position on the issue at hand. Finally, a comprehensive index allows readers to locate content quickly and efficiently.

Introducing Issues with Opposing Viewpoints is also significantly different from Opposing Viewpoints. As the series title implies, its presentation will help introduce students to the concept of opposing viewpoints, and learn to use this material to aid in critical writing and debate. The series' four-color, accessible format makes the books attractive and inviting to readers of all levels. In addition, each viewpoint has been carefully edited to maximize a reader's understanding of the content. Short but thorough viewpoints capture the essence of an argument. A substantial, thought-provoking essay question placed at the end of each viewpoint asks the student to further investigate the issues raised in the viewpoint, compare and contrast two authors' arguments, or consider how one might go about forming an opinion on the topic at hand. Each viewpoint contains sidebars that include at-a-glance information and handy statistics. A Facts About section located in the back of the book further supplies students with relevant facts and figures.

Following in the tradition of the Opposing Viewpoints series, Greenhaven Press continues to provide readers with invaluable exposure to the controversial issues that shape our world. As John Stuart Mill once wrote: "The only way in which a human being can make some approach to knowing the whole of a subject is by hearing what can be said about it by persons of every variety of opinion and studying all modes in which it can be looked at by every character of mind. No wise man ever acquired his wisdom in any mode but this." It is to this principle that Introducing Issues with Opposing Viewpoints books are dedicated.

Introduction

"Our country's all-volunteer force attracts idealistic and committed young Americans. They stay in service longer because they have chosen the military life. The result is a military with the highest level of training and experience, motivation, and professionalism."

—President George W. Bush

"How can we in good conscience keep asking the same insufficient number of brave soldiers and Marines to carry on a seemingly endless fight that lacks a full national effort to succeed?"

—Author Herb Field

On June 30, 1973, as the Vietnam War was wrapping up after nine grueling years, the United States drafted its last soldier. The next day the U.S. government launched the All-Volunteer Force (AVF)—an initiative aimed at maintaining a strong military without forcing young men to serve. The thinking behind the AVF's creation was that people who served by choice would be more motivated, better qualified, and more committed than those who were called into service. In the years since the establishment of an all-volunteer service, opinions have varied widely about whether it has helped or hindered America's military readiness and whether it is the best option for meeting the military challenges of the twenty-first century.

The draft has had its opponents since it was first used during the Civil War. But because it was understood that a strong military was essential for national defense, wartime drafts were by and large accepted and even actively supported. The Vietnam War, however, was different and was one of the key factors in driving the federal government toward an all-volunteer military. Initially met with popular support, the war soon overwhelmed military forces not used to fighting guerilla forces in jungle terrain. Between 1964 and 1973, nearly 2.6 million Americans served in the war; of those, more than 57,000 were killed. Vietnam consumed the Johnson administration, and the frustration carried into the Nixon administration. As casualties rose, and with no real progress evident, public support for the war dwindled; peace movements were organized at college campuses across the country, and antiwar riots broke out in major American cities for the first time since the Civil War. Early in 1975 the South Vietnamese capital, Saigon, was captured by North Vietnamese troops. Walter Cronkite—the longtime CBS anchor known as "the most trusted man in America"—pronounced the war "unwinnable."

In 1969 President Richard M. Nixon convened a special commission, headed by former defense secretary Thomas S. Gates Jr., to determine whether an all-volunteer military was feasible. The Gates Commission concluded in 1970 that an all-volunteer force would be preferable to a draft because those who joined would be doing so

Young men are sworn in to the army after being drafted for the Vietnam War in 1967. Hundreds of thousands of soldiers were forced to serve under the draft system.

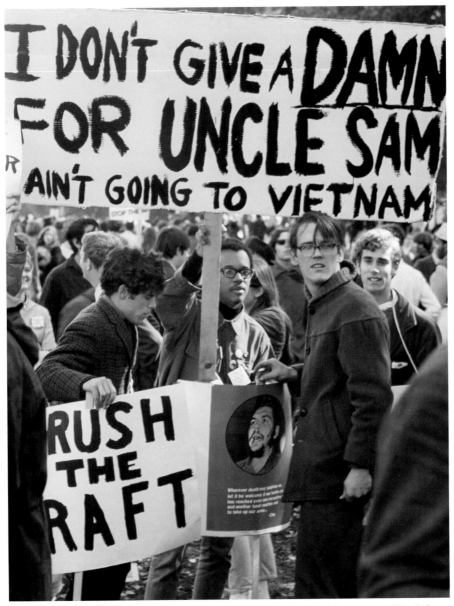

Protesters oppose the Vietnam War at a 1967 rally. Opposition to the Vietnam War led to the abolition of the draft in 1973.

because they wanted to join. The question was whether enough people could be convinced that joining the military was rewarding. To ensure that enough people would volunteer to maintain an adequate military, the Gates Commission recommended that recruiting efforts be increased and entry-level pay be raised. In 1972 Congress raised

The Draft Around the World

These countries have a strict draft requiring military service with little exception.

Afghanistan	Georgia	Morocco
Albania	Greece	Mozambique
Algeria	Guatemala	North Korea
Angola	Guinea	Paraguay
Bolivia	Guinea-Bissau	Peru
Cambodia	Honduras	Philippines
Chile	Iran	Romania
China	Iraq	Singapore
Colombia	Israel	Somalia
Cuba	Kazakhstan	South Korea
Dominican Republic	Laos	Sudan
Ecuador	Lebanon	Thailand
Egypt	Liberia	Tunisia
El Salvador	Libya	Turkey
Equatorial Guinea	Madagascar	Venezuela
Estonia	Mexico	Vietnam
Ethiopia	Mongolia	Yemen

Source: Office of the United Nations High Commissioner for Human Rights, 2001.

the pay of first-time enlisted men by more than 60 percent. The different branches of the military revamped their recruitment strategies to emphasize the value of military training and experience in the civilian world. Patriotism was still emphasized as well—but for the first time the military highlighted ways in which service would tangibly benefit the individual recruit. Slogans like the army's "Be All That You Can Be" underscored the scope of opportunities that awaited volunteers.

More than thirty years after the AVF's creation, has it worked? According to the Bush administration, it has. The scope of opportunities for today's recruits alone has made the military a more attractive option for young men and women. A senior Defense Department official explained during a briefing on the AVF that "in the draft era, we largely told you what was good for you . . . 'you're going to like this military occupation . . . it builds character.' Now we come to [recruits] and say, 'Well, which of these . . . training opportunities would entice you to join and stay with us?'" Indeed, the military of the twenty-first century offers volunteers the chance to learn in depth about computers, engineering, heavy industrial equipment—experiences that transfer to the private sector.

But the military of the twenty-first century is also forced to deal with warfare that, unlike past battles, has no clearly defined beginning and end. The terrorist threat, especially in the Middle East, is as foreign to American troops today as jungle guerilla warfare was in the 1960s. And while a recruit who volunteers for military service understands that service during wartime can mean exposure to extreme danger, their conventional combat training may not prepare them for just how extreme current dangers can be.

Charles A. Krohn, a professor at the University of Michigan and a former deputy chief of public affairs for the army, expressed his concern about the AVF in June 2005. "The Gates Commission, in considering the transition from a draft to a volunteer force, optimistically assumed that young Americans would come to the colors if the

Army volunteers are indoctrinated for service at a 2005 ceremony. Some argue that volunteers make better soldiers because they are truly motivated to serve their country.

nation went to war with any country that presented a conventional threat. Unconventional, non-state warfare didn't enter into the commission's calculus." Others, such as *New York Times* op-ed columnist Bob Herbert, have been more blunt in assessing the all-volunteer system: "The all-volunteer army is fine in peacetime, and in military routs like the first gulf war. But when the troops are locked in a prolonged war that yields high casualties, and they look over their shoulders to see if reinforcements are coming from the general population, they find—as they're finding now—that no one is there."

Whether the United States needs a military draft is a highly emotional debate, but there are rational arguments on both sides of the issue. The viewpoints presented in *Introducing Issues with Opposing Viewpoints: Military Draft,* offer a variety of thought-provoking observations and insights that can help students better understand this complex topic.

Chapter 1

Should a Military Draft Be Reinstated?

It is hotly debated whether an all-volunteer force can adequately meet America's military needs in the modern world.

Viewpoint

1

The United States Needs a Draft

Phillip Carter and Paul Glastris

"A 21st-century draft . . . would create a cascading series of benefits for society."

Compulsory military service has been used successfully in the United States several times since the Civil War. In the following piece, Phillip Carter and Paul Glastris contend that a draft, structured properly and with an eye toward service options besides combat, can strengthen the current military force. Moreover, they say, it can instill a sense of civic duty in young Americans and spur them to develop creative ways to serve their country, whether on a national or a neighborhood level.

Phillip Carter is an attorney and former army captain. Paul Glastris is editor in chief of the *Washington Monthly*.

AS YOU READ, CONSIDER THE FOLLOWING QUESTIONS:

1. According to the authors, how would a draft affect both rich and poor Americans?
2. What do the authors suggest the government require of four-year colleges and universities?
3. What benefits do the authors think a new draft can bring to the U.S. home front?

Phillip Carter and Paul Glastris, "The Case for the Draft," *Washington Monthly,* vol. 37, March 2005, pp. 18–25. Copyright © 2005 by Washington Monthly Publishing, LLC, 733 Fifteenth St. NW, Ste. 520, Washington, DC 20005, (202) 393-5155. Web site: www.washingtonmonthly.com. Reproduced by permission.

America's all-volunteer military simply cannot deploy and sustain enough troops to succeed in places like Iraq while still deterring threats elsewhere in the world. Simply adding more soldiers to the active duty force, as some in Washington are now suggesting, may sound like a good solution. But it's not, for sound operational and pragmatic reasons. America doesn't need a bigger standing army; it needs a deep bench of trained soldiers held in reserve who can be mobilized to handle the unpredictable but inevitable wars and humanitarian interventions of the future. And while there are several ways the all-volunteer force can create some extra surge capacity, all of them are limited.

A Draft for a New Era

The only effective solution to the manpower crunch is the one America has turned to again and again in its history: the draft. Not the mass combat mobilizations of World War II, nor the inequitable conscription of Vietnam—for just as threats change and war-fighting advances, so too must the draft. A modernized draft would demand that the privileged participate. It would give all who serve a choice over how

Draftees wait to be processed for the Vietnam War in 1968. Some experts believe that reinstating the draft would instill a sense of civic duty in young people.

they serve. And it would provide the military, on a "just in time" basis, large numbers of deployable ground troops, particularly the peacekeepers we'll need to meet the security challenges of the 21st century. . . .

[There is one way to provide] the military with sufficient numbers of high-quality, deployable ground forces: conscription. America has nearly always chosen this option to staff its military in times of war. Today, no leading politician in either party will come anywhere near the idea—the draft having replaced Social Security as the third rail of American politics. This will have to change if the United States is to remain the world's preeminent power.

Addressing the Challenges of Conscription

Traditional conscription has its obvious downsides. On a practical level, draftees tend to be less motivated than volunteers. Because they serve for relatively short periods of time (typically two years), any investment made in their training is lost to the military once the draftees return to civilian life. And despite the current manpower

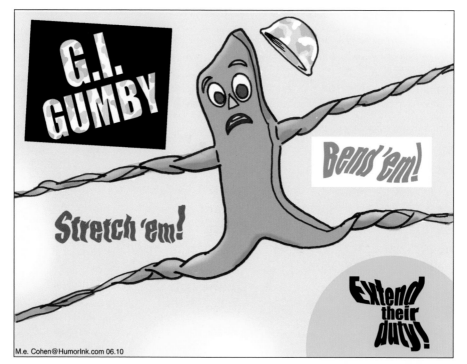

M.E. Cohen. Copyright © 2004 by M.E. Cohen. Reproduced by permission of Cagle Cartoons, Inc.

Soldiers take the Oath of Enlistment, a vow to serve their country with honor.

shortage, there's no foreseeable scenario in which all 28 million young Americans currently of draft age would be needed.

Above all else, there's the serious ethical problem that conscription means government compelling young adults to risk death, and to kill—an act of the state that seems contrary to the basic notions of liberty which animate our society.

In practice, however, our republic has decided many times throughout its history that a draft was necessary to protect those basic liberties. Even if you disagreed with the decision to [invade] Iraq, or think the president's rhetoric is demagogic and his policies disastrous, it is hard to argue that Islamic terrorism isn't a threat to freedom and security, at home and abroad. Moreover, any American, liberal or conservative, ought to have moral qualms about basing our nation's security on an all-volunteer force drawn disproportionately, as ours is, from America's lower socioeconomic classes. And the cost of today's war is being borne by an extremely narrow slice of America. Camp Pendleton,

California, home to the 1st Marine Expeditionary Force, is also home to approximately one-seventh of the U.S. fatalities from Iraq. In theory, our democracy will not fight unpopular wars because the people who must bear the casualties can impose their will on our elected leaders to end a war they do not support. But when such a small fraction of America shoulders the burden—and pays the cost—of America's wars, this democratic system breaks down.

Nor are the practical considerations of a draft impossible to overcome. A draft lottery, of the kind that existed in the peacetime draft of the 1950s, with no exemptions for college students, would provide the military an appropriate and manageable amount of manpower without the class inequities that poisoned the national culture during Vietnam. Such a system, however, would not avoid the problem of flooding the military with less-than-fully motivated conscripts.

A Wide Range of Options for Service

A better solution would fix the weaknesses of the all-volunteer force without undermining its strengths. Here's how such a plan might work. Instead of a lottery, the federal government would impose a requirement that no four-year college or university be allowed to accept a student, male or female, unless and until that student had completed a twelve-month to two-year term of service. Unlike an old-fashioned draft, this 21st-century service requirement would provide a vital element of personal choice. Students could choose to fulfill their obligations in any of three ways: in national service programs like AmeriCorps (tutoring disadvantaged children), in homeland security assignments (guarding ports), or in the military. Those who chose the latter could serve as military police officers, truck drivers, or other non-combat specialists requiring only modest levels of training. (It should be noted that the Army currently offers two-year enlistments for all of these jobs, as well as for the infantry.) They would be deployed as needed for peacekeeping or nation-building missions. They would serve for twelve months to two years, with modest follow-on reserve obligations.

Whichever option they choose, all who serve would receive modest stipends and GI Bill-type college grants. Those who sign up for lengthier and riskier duty, however, would receive higher pay and larger college grants. Most would no doubt pick the less dangerous options. But some would certainly select the military—out of patriotism, a sense of adven-

Reinstating the draft could help take pressure off of overworked soldiers and a thinly stretched military.

ture, or to test their mettle. Even if only 10 percent of the 1-million young people who annually start at four-year colleges and universities were to choose the military option, the armed forces would receive 100,000 fresh recruits every year. These would be motivated recruits, having chosen the military over other, less demanding forms of service. And because they would all be college-grade and college-bound, they would have—to a greater extent than your average volunteer recruit—the savvy and inclination to pick up foreign languages and other skills that are often the key to effective peacekeeping work.

A Wealth of Benefits

A 21st-century draft like this would create a cascading series of benefits for society. It would instill a new ethic of service in that sector of society, the college-bound, most likely to reap the fruits of American prosperity. It would mobilize an army of young people for vital domestic missions, such as helping a growing population of seniors who want to avoid nursing homes but need help with simple daily tasks like grocery shopping. It would give more of America's elite an experience of the military. Above all, it would provide the all-important surge capacity now missing from our force structure, insuring that the military would never again lack for manpower. And it would do all this without requiring any American to carry a gun who did not choose to do so.

The war in Iraq has shown us, and the world, many things: the bloody costs of inept leadership; the courage of the average American soldier; the hunger for democracy among some of the earth's most oppressed people. But perhaps more than anything, Iraq has shown that our military power has limits. As currently constituted, the U.S. military can win the wars, but it cannot win the peace, nor can it commit for the long term to the stability and security of a nation such as Iraq. Our enemies have learned this, and they will use that knowledge to their advantage in the next war to tie us down and bleed us until we lose the political will to fight.

If America wishes to retain its mantle of global leadership, it must develop a military force structure capable of persevering under these circumstances. Fortunately, we know how to build such a force. We have done it many times in the past. The question is: Do we have the will to do so again?

EVALUATING THE AUTHORS' ARGUMENTS:

The authors of this viewpoint believe that a military draft can benefit the armed forces and the United States. They offer specific suggestions for how to improve the draft. What is your opinion of these suggestions? Do you think they are realistic or far-fetched? Explain.

The United States Does Not Need a Draft

"I don't know anyone in the executive branch of the government who believes that it would be appropriate or necessary to reinstitute the draft."

Donald H. Rumsfeld

In the following viewpoint, U.S. secretary of defense Donald H. Rumsfeld argues that the current number of service members and reservists is adequate to defend the nation. Rumsfeld believes that the way to make the military more efficient is to find ways to streamline operations, not to add more soldiers, sailors, and pilots. Moreover, he contends, some administrative work could be handled by civilians, cutting down on the numbers of military personnel. By freeing these servicepeople from bureaucratic duty and assigning them more specific military tasks, the volunteer armed forces will function more effectively and without a need to expand the ranks.

As secretary of defense since 2001, Donald H. Rumsfeld has directed the U.S. response to the September 11 terrorist attacks. He also served as secretary of defense from 1975–1977 under President Gerald Ford.

Donald H. Rumsfeld, "Remarks to the Newspaper Association of America/American Society of Newspaper Editors," Washington, DC, April 22, 2004.

1. Why does Rumsfeld feel that training more people to serve in the military may not be an efficient way to make the armed forces stronger?
2. How many men and women are on active duty, according to the author?
3. What does Rumsfeld mean by his analogy of a water keg and a spigot?

I don't know anyone in the executive branch of the government who believes that it would be appropriate or necessary to reinstitute the draft.

We have a very large population. We have a relatively small military. We have been very successful in recruiting and retaining the people we need. There were a lot of difficulties with the draft, as people may recall. . . . There was a draft, but a relatively small number of . . . the male population in that age group was ever drafted. A large number were exempted because they were married or they were teachers or they were students or they were [a member of another category that] . . . society decided to set aside and not draft.

The result of it was that we conscripted people and trained them, and then they had relatively short periods of service. And they did a great job. But the task of training that large volume of people relative to the relatively small number who actually stayed in the service for a sustained period, from a cost-benefit standpoint, was useful to do during a certain part of our history, but we believe is not useful to do at the present time. . . .

> ## FAST FACT
>
> In 2006 the U.S. Army raised the maximum enlistment age for both regular and reserve components from forty to forty-two as a way to draw from a larger pool of recruits.

Sustaining a Viable Force

How do we sustain a force we need to engage in the kinds of activities that our country's engaged in? I mean, you think about it, we've got close to 2,000 people in Haiti, and they'll be there probably another month until the U.N. force replaces them. We had some folks in Liberia, and we have people in Korea. We have people in Bosnia and Kosovo—Bosnia's running down this year—to say nothing of the ones that I've mentioned involved in the global war on terror and elsewhere in the world. So one can make the question, what do you do? How do you sustain what you need to sustain?

Let me put it this way. General [Peter] Schoomaker, the chief of staff for the Army, says think of a water keg that's that high. And what we've got is we've got 1.4 million men and women in uniform on active duty, and if you add all the reserves—the selective and the individual ready reserves—it comes up over 2 million people. . . . All we're trying to do is sustain 135,000 in Iraq plus the other commitments I mentioned.

Secretary of Defense Donald H. Rumsfeld (left) talks with lieutenants in the U.S. Navy about his belief that a draft is unnecessary.

No Reason in the World for a Draft

Now, if that's a stress on the force, that probably means you've got to do one of [two] things. You either have to increase the size of the water keg or you have to move the spigot down. At the present time we're only accessing a very small portion of the two-plus million men and women in the active force and the reserves in our current deployments. So the question is, why is that? And the answer is because the spigot's too high. We need to lower the spigot. We don't need to get a bigger barrel.

There isn't any reason in the world why we can't manage this force better with less stress on it, and it simply requires changing the rules, changing the requirements, changing the regulations in ways that we can manage that force considerably better. And that is the process that

Fran. Copyright © by Fran. Reproduced by permission.

An officer inspects a house during a raid in Iraq. Such missions require specialized, highly skilled soldiers who are attracted to the all-volunteer force.

the Army's engaged in. They're doing an excellent job at it. The chief of staff for the Army is hopeful that he's going to be able to, for example, go from thirty-three brigades up to forty-three or forty-eight brigades without a permanent increase in the size of the force, and that's by better utilizing the people we have. I don't know if he'll make it, but he's a terrific leader and he's working hard on it and he believes that's doable. Well, now, that's a significant increase in combat capability.

Assigning Jobs More Intelligently

We have some 300,000, I'm told, men and women in uniform doing things that are tasks that need not be done by military personnel. Now why is that? The reason we have military personnel doing tasks that are not military . . . is because we have, I don't know, dozens and dozens of different personnel systems and we're not capable of managing our civil service in a way that is efficient.

So when a person in the Pentagon has a problem and they need someone to solve something, rather than reaching for a civil service person, they reach for a uniformed person because they can bring him on, they can send him away, they can deploy him, they can train him, and they can manage it in an efficient way. Or they reach for a contractor. They can sign a contract that fits the current needs, and they can stop the contract when they want it over. So we end up with three hundred—we're not using our civil service the way we ought to. They're terrific people. There isn't any reason, with the right rules under this new national security personnel system we just got . . . we can't manage them better and use them properly and end up with some fraction of that 300,000 people in uniform that are doing civilian jobs, some fraction of those moved out of civilian jobs back into military jobs so that we'll have them available to reduce stress on the force.

EVALUATING THE AUTHORS' ARGUMENTS:

The author draws on his years of government experience to make his case against a draft. He believes that adding more people without a workable plan or adequate resources will make the military less able to do its job well. Contrast Rumsfeld's points with Phillip Carter and Paul Glastris's arguments in the previous viewpoint. Do you think Rumsfeld's concept of a leaner, more efficient military would boost morale among those currently serving? Why?

A Draft Will Revitalize the Military

"It is irresponsible to continue to attempt to meet current military commitments and threats without a draft."

Herb Field

In the following article, Herb Field argues that a return to a military draft is the only way to keep the appropriate number of qualified military personnel. With recruitment numbers down and opposition to the war in Iraq growing stronger, the only way to maintain a wartime army is to add troops. Moreover, the draft will provide much-needed relief for those currently serving beyond their original tours of duty. Exhausted troops can finally go home while fresh replacements take charge.

Herb Field is an editorial writer for the *Patriot-News* in Harrisburg, Pennsylvania.

AS YOU READ, CONSIDER THE FOLLOWING QUESTIONS:

1. In Field's view, why has the military been unable to send soldiers home after two or even three tours of battlefield duty?
2. According to the author, why would a shorter enlistment requirement fail to add the necessary resources to the army?
3. How well would today's military be able to deal with new conflicts given the current size and enlistment numbers, according to Field?

The handwriting is on the wall. In big, bold letters. Bring back the draft.

There is no other responsible choice. Not if we are going to continue as we are in Iraq and Afghanistan, pursuing President Bush's "freedom" initiative to liberate the world's oppressed, and, by the way, defend the country from real external dangers, such as the likes of North Korea.

You can't keep sending the same soldiers and Marines back to the battlefields, with some on their third rotation. There aren't enough of them now. And recruitment for the all-volunteer Army hasn't been this low since it was conceived in the 1970s. The Army met only 68 percent of its recruitment target in March [2005], 73 percent in February, with the head of recruitment, Maj. Gen. Michael Rochelle, saying this is "the toughest recruiting climate we've ever faced."

Recruiting Efforts Falling Short

And it isn't as if Army recruiters aren't trying. In fact, they've been trying too hard, pushing the ethical limits in so many instances to entice

A soldier talks with a potential recruit about army life. With recruitment at an all-time low, some have looked to the draft as a way to meet America's service needs.

Looking Back at the Draft

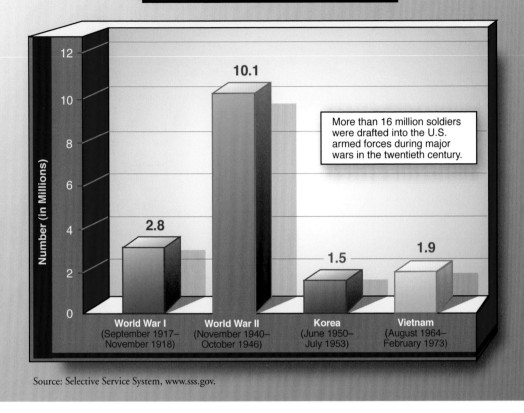

More than 16 million soldiers were drafted into the U.S. armed forces during major wars in the twentieth century.

Number (in Millions)

World War I (September 1917– November 1918)	World War II (November 1940– October 1946)	Korea (June 1950– July 1953)	Vietnam (August 1964– February 1973)
2.8	10.1	1.5	1.9

Source: Selective Service System, www.sss.gov.

young people to sign up that Rochelle . . . ordered a nationwide one-day "values stand down.". . . This [was] intended to reintroduce the Army's 7,500 recruiters to rules that prohibit lying to applicants or suppressing information that would make a recruit ineligible.

The Army needs to find 80,000 new soldiers [in 2005] and threatens to fall well short of that number. Secretary of Defense Donald Rumsfeld created a "blue-to-green" program to encourage Air Force and Navy personnel to switch to the Army, but it isn't drawing many takers. Now, the Army has announced that it will offer an enlistment for only fifteen months in the regular Army, after which there would be a two-year commitment in either the National Guard or Army Reserve. But how enticing is that, with thousands of Guard and Reserve members serving in Iraq and Afghanistan?

Congress will begin consideration . . . of raising the Army complement by 10,000 soldiers over Pentagon objections, but that would still be far from adequate, even if you could get them to sign up.

Iraqis are increasingly victimized due to a failure to secure their country. Instituting a draft could provide enough troops to stabilize Iraq.

So, we need to bring back the draft. How else to ensure a sufficient supply of troops for the defense of the country? How else to carry on Bush's various foreign ventures and back up his tough talk? How else to awaken the country to the bloody mess we are in? And how else to get those in power who support these policies to actually confront the reality of war and the sacrifices it should demand of them and their loved ones, not just the few who are bearing the entire burden of foreign policies that are long on rhetoric and short on common sense.

Longer, Bloodier Wars

It is irresponsible to continue to attempt to meet current military commitments and threats without a draft. [In May 2005] Gen. Richard Myers, chairman of the Joint Chiefs of Staff, warned Congress in a report that operations in Iraq and Afghanistan limited the military's ability to deal with other potential conflicts. He said U.S. forces would still succeed but the wars would be longer and bloodier than previously predicted.

But I don't expect this administration to take the difficult, but responsible course. To seek to reinstate the draft would be a political disaster. It would be to admit that mistakes—huge mistakes—were made. It would be to acknowledge that we are pursuing a deeply flawed foreign policy that is heavy on a military apparatus nearing its breaking point, and woefully lacking in big-league diplomacy.

On the other hand, how can we in good conscience keep asking the same insufficient number of brave soldiers and Marines to carry on a seemingly endless fight that lacks a full national effort to succeed?

EVALUATING THE AUTHOR'S ARGUMENTS:

The author, while clearly not in support of the Bush administration or the war in Iraq, believes nonetheless that the only fair way to lessen the burden on those currently fighting is to add to the ranks through a military draft. Given his arguments and the evidence he provides about falling recruitment numbers, do you think that reinstating the draft would boost the morale of those serving and instill patriotism in those called to serve? Why or why not?

A Draft Will Lower the Quality of the Military

Nathaniel Fick

"Renewing the draft would be a blow against the men and women in uniform, a dumbing down of the institution they serve."

Nathaniel Fick is a former marine officer and the author of *One Bullet Away: The Making of a Marine Officer.* In the following viewpoint Fick argues that the all-volunteer army is an effective force of committed professionals, highly skilled soldiers, sailors, and pilots who serve by choice. Implementing a draft, he argues, would populate the ranks with people who lack the specific skills and commitment necessary to become effective soldiers. Fick concludes that the government should devote its efforts to attracting and recruiting skilled and talented people rather than opening the military doors to unqualified or unwilling people who would be a liability in combat.

AS YOU READ, CONSIDER THE FOLLOWING QUESTIONS:

1. How long does it take for a soldier to become an effective combat fighter, according to the author?

2. What conclusions does the author draw about the number of diverse backgrounds among his fellow marines?
3. According to Fick, what is the best way to enlarge the volunteer military without reinstating the draft?

I went to war as a believer in the citizen-soldier. My college study of the classics idealized Greeks who put down their plows for swords, returning to their fields at the end of the war. As a marine officer in Afghanistan and Iraq, however, I learned that the victors on today's battlefields are long-term, professional soldiers. Thus the increasing calls for reinstating the draft . . . are well intentioned but misguided. Imposing a draft on the military I served in would harm it grievously for years.

Serving Is a Labor of Love

I led platoons of volunteers. In Afghanistan, my marines slept each night in holes they hacked from the rocky ground. They carried hundred-pound packs in addition to their fears of minefields and ambushes, their homesickness, loneliness and exhaustion. The most junior did it for $964.80 per month. They didn't complain, and I never wrestled with discipline problems. Each and every marine wanted to be there. If anyone hadn't, he would have been a drain on the platoon and a liability in combat.

In Iraq, I commanded a reconnaissance platoon, the marines' special operations force. Many of my enlisted marines were college-educated; some had been to graduate school. All had volunteered once for the marines, again for the infantry, and a third time for recon. They were proud to serve as part of an elite unit. Like most demanding professionals, they were their own harshest critics, intolerant of their peers whose performance fell short.

> **FAST FACT**
>
> A 2004 poll conducted by the Alliance for Security found that 52 percent of those eligible for the draft would either actively seek deferment or refuse to serve.

The Military Needs a Skilled Tactical Force

The dumb grunt is an anachronism. He has been replaced by the strategic corporal. Immense firepower and improved technology have pushed decision-making with national consequences down to individual enlisted men. Modern warfare requires that even the most junior infantryman master a wide array of technical and tactical skills.

Honing these skills to reflex, a prerequisite for survival in combat, takes time—a year of formal training and another year of on-the-job experience were generally needed to transform my young marines into competent warriors. The Marine Corps demands four-year active enlistments because it takes that long to train troops and ensure those

Fran. Copyright © by Fran. Reproduced by permission.

Highly trained soldiers perform surveillance for air traffic control over Baghdad. Retaining skilled soldiers is part of the appeal of the all-volunteer force.

training dollars are put to use in the field. One- or two-year terms, the longest that would be likely under conscription, would simply not allow for this comprehensive training. . . .

The Military Can Grow Without a Draft

[One] argument most often advanced for a renewed draft is that the military is too small to meet its commitments. Absolutely true. But the armed forces are stretched thin not from a lack of volunteers but because Congress and the Pentagon are not willing to spend the money to expand the force. Each of the services met or exceeded its recruiting goals in 2003, and the numbers have increased across the board [in 2004]. Even the Army National Guard, often cited as the abused beast of burden in Iraq, has seen re-enlistments soar past its goal, 65 percent, to 141 percent (the figure is greater than 100 because many guardsmen are re-enlisting early).

Expanding the military to meet additional responsibilities is a matter of structural change: if we build it, they will come. And build it we must. Many of my marines are already on their third combat deployment in the global war on terrorism; they will need replacing. Increasing the size of the active-duty military would lighten the burden on every soldier, sailor, airman and marine. Paradoxically, a larger military becomes more sustainable than a smaller one: fewer combat deployments improves service members' quality of life and contributes to higher rates of enlistment and retention. . . .

Retain the Quality of the Military

The current volunteer force rejects applicants who score poorly on its entrance aptitude exam, disclose a history of significant drug use or suffer from any of a number of orthopedic or chronic injuries. Face it: any unwilling draftee could easily find a way to fail any of these tests. The military, then, would be left either to abandon its standards and accept all comers, or to remain true to them and allow the draft to become volunteerism by another name. Stripped of its volunteer ideology, but still unable to compel service from dissenters, the military would end up weaker and less representative than the volunteer force—the very opposite of the draft's intended goals.

Renewing the draft would be a blow against the men and women in uniform, a dumbing down of the institution they serve. The United States military exists to win battles, not to test social policy. Enlarging the volunteer force would show our soldiers that Americans recognize their hardship and are willing to pay the bill to help them better protect the nation. My view of the citizen-soldier was altered, but not destroyed, in combat. We cannot all pick up the sword, nor should we be forced to—but we owe our support to those who do.

> **EVALUATING THE AUTHOR'S ARGUMENTS:**
>
> The author of this viewpoint served as an officer in the U.S. Marine Corps in the wars in Afghanistan and Iraq. How does his experience influence your opinion of his argument? Explain your answer.

Chapter 2

How Will a Draft Affect Society?

Gender, race, and class are key issues that appear in debates about the draft.

A Draft Can Unify the Nation

"Over time, everyone would have served, giving us a shared national experience that would pull the nation together."

William R. King

William R. King is University Professor in the Katz School of Business at the University of Pittsburgh. In the following viewpoint, King explores the potential unifying benefits of reinstating a military draft. The current, inequitable volunteer system, King argues, not only puts the poor at a disadvantage, it also gives no incentives to the rich. He contends that the draft, used as part of a "universal national service" program, would instill a sense of commitment and community in young people. By encouraging and developing this sense of commitment, King concludes, many young people would find military service an appealing option and an excellent way to give back to society.

AS YOU READ, CONSIDER THE FOLLOWING QUESTIONS:
1. According to the author, what class of people do the fighting in Iraq?
2. Describe the national service program proposed by the author.
3. Why, according to King, would young people choose the military as part of their national service requirement?

I've [recently] had the occasion to chat with six people who told me that their child was serving with the military in Iraq. Each of them volunteered the information and all spoke proudly of their kids.

Subsequently I reflected on these coincidental brief conversations with a security guard, a lawn service guy, a police officer, a janitor, a store clerk and a nurse.

My reflections led me to realize, in my gut, because I'd always known it in my head, that the Iraq war is being fought by the children of workers. During that same period, I've had many conversations with professors, business executives and professionals—and none of them has made any similar mention of their kids in the military. Their children are simply not doing the job being done by the children of the "working class."

As we enter [another] year of what is going to be a long period of engagement of our military with terrorists, I think that we need to

One concern about the all-volunteer force is that it pulls too heavily from the working class.

question the fairness of this. We need to examine how the people who serve are chosen and whether our society should be concerned with the equity that is involved with our "volunteer army."

The Difference Between Wartime and Peacetime

The children of educated, well-to-do families have little motivation to volunteer. They have options—college, training courses or good jobs. Children who graduate from high school without such prospects find that there are significant incentives offered by the military—enlistment bonuses, training in skills that have potential for civilian jobs, money for college when their service is completed, travel and decent pay.

In peacetime, this is inequitable, but perhaps best overall. The money, training and educational opportunities that are offered benefit kids who probably would never be able to otherwise obtain them. The military, as it has for many decades, serves as a vehicle for raising youngsters out of poverty and for opening up new horizons for kids whose range of vision is limited.

However, in wartime, these benefits may be outweighed by the inequitable distribution of the costs and risks.

Sandy Huffaker. Copyright © 2003 by Sandy Huffaker. Reproduced by permission of Cagle Cartoons, Inc.

What can we do about this? Since the military is not meeting its recruiting goals, one obvious answer is to reinstate the draft. However, the draft, even when it was conducted on a lottery basis, was also inequitable because it was full of deferments and because it left people feeling lucky or unlucky.

Universal National Service?

During the late Vietnam War, I studied this problem as a senior staff member for U.S. Senator Sam Nunn. I concluded, and he agreed, that a universal national service program was the solution. Such a program would require that every able American perform a period of national service upon attaining the age of eighteen or on high school graduation, whichever comes later.

Of course, there are far too many kids who would become available each year than the military could possibly absorb, so how could this plan be made to be feasible? We worked out a proposal that made it both feasible and economic. The senator's proposed bill involved having many different service opportunities beyond the military made available. National servers could tutor kids in urban and rural areas; [or] they could work with the disabled, the aged and the sick, providing services that cannot be otherwise afforded.

Let's Solve Many Social Problems

These diverse opportunities could be organized by civilian service organizations and operated by their local branches, which would allow many servers to live at home during their service. The required expenditures would replace those for existing federal programs such as youth job training, welfare for the relevant age group and existing service programs.

Unfortunately, the law that was enacted was only a pale imitation of our proposal. It created a small, voluntary program that did not include a military option.

Drawing soldiers from all corners of society could help foster national pride and unity.

I have maintained my monitoring of this idea over the years and been in close contact with the group of analysts who believe, as I do, that a universal national service program would solve many of our societal problems, give young people a learning opportunity at a critical stage in their lives, and solve the current military enlistment deficiency on a basis that is equitable.

This is so because national service jobs could be designed so that they are not taking work away from paid workers. They could focus on things that aren't otherwise likely to get done at all.

Conscription Would Build National Pride

All of the tasks done by national servers would involve significant training so that skills are developed to complement the positive feelings about themselves that would come with performing meaningful jobs that help others. At this age, most kids naturally want to do good for others and the country needs to give them an opportunity and take advantage of their inclinations.

If young people are given the option of choosing among alternative ways to serve, many will choose the military—not because they are given tangible incentives, but because they are patriotic and want the adventure and travel that the military offers. This would be true of affluent kids as well as poorer ones.

Such a program would ask every young person to "give something back" to a country and society that has given much to all of us. The satisfaction that this would engender in young people would raise their self-esteem in a way that few other things could possibly accomplish. Over time, everyone would have served, giving us a shared national experience that would pull the nation together.

A national service program is as relevant today as it was then, perhaps more so. It would do a great deal of good for our society and importantly, it would be fair to all.

EVALUATING THE AUTHOR'S ARGUMENTS:

King believes that a reinstatement of the military draft, as part of a broader national service program, would give young people a sense of self-worth and a desire to give back to the community. Based on his arguments, do you think a national service program would create a shared sense of community service and giving—and do you think more young people would choose military service? Why?

A Draft Will Not Unify the Nation

Murray Polner

"The truth is, no draft can ever be fair."

In the following viewpoint, writer Murray Polner argues that the all-volunteer force has been stretched so tightly that it cannot continue to fight effectively. He does not see the draft as a means of expanding or improving the military. Rather, he believes that, based on the history of the draft in the United States, wealthy and well-connected young men and women will find ways to exempt themselves from service, while those with no influence will be compelled to serve and risk their lives, often prolonging ill-advised conflicts initiated by policy makers who themselves have never served in any military capacity.

Murray Polner is an editor at the History News Network (HNN).

AS YOU READ, CONSIDER THE FOLLOWING QUESTIONS:
1. Who, according to the author, is likely to determine where the United States will have a military presence in the future?
2. In the author's opinion, did draftees fare better or worse than military professionals in World Wars I and II, the Korean conflict, and Vietnam?
3. Why does Polner believe today's policy makers are unqualified to make decisions about a possible draft?

Murray Polner, "A Military Draft After the Elections?" Veterans for Common Sense, www.veteransfor commonsense.org, September 24, 2004. Reproduced by permission of the author.

The war in Iraq has not been a "cakewalk" as was widely trumpeted by its promoters in the months leading up to the American invasion. And if, as [Secretary of Defense] Donald Rumsfeld once said, Iraq turns out to be "a long hard slog" (it has) who then will be called on to do the slogging?

It is fair to ask how many wars this nation can fight with its hard-pressed volunteer forces, many of whom are now forbidden to leave when their enlistments run out. Or when they are finally released, how many will re-enlist. A more pressing question is, how many of you may be forced to fight and perhaps die for imperial dreams concocted by a small clique of extremely influential neoconservatives and jingoists, very few of whom have ever served in the military?

And even more ominously: There is increasing chatter in Washington among neoconservatives and their favored columnists of even more wars ahead. They call it spreading their version of democracy; we call it more aggressive and unjustifiable wars. It is being suggested that America's next targets should be Iran, Syria and North Korea.

This time Selective Service System regulations have been changed. This time, as SSS states, "a college student could have his induction postponed only until the end of the current semester. A senior could be postponed until the end of the full academic year."

Canada will no longer welcome you. A new SSS plan, obtained under the Freedom of Information Act by the *Seattle Post Intelligencer* [in May 2004], proposes raising the age of draft registration to thirty-four years old, up from twenty-five, and possibly including women as well. People with special skills, such as computers, foreign languages, medical training and the like, will also be subject to being drafted. In effect, *if approved,* it will be a universal draft where everyone, including the kids of the rich and powerful, will *allegedly* be eligible to serve in the military.

Vice President Dick Cheney watches a U.S. military reenlistment ceremony. Cheney and other administration officials do not believe a draft is necessary at this time.

Will a Draft Actually Make Everyone Serve Equally?

But remember this: No congressional son was drafted during the Vietnam War and today there are virtually no congressional sons or daughters serving as enlisted combat personnel in Iraq. Since 9/11 it is almost impossible to name a single prominent pro-war activist, those who demand an all-out war against terrorism, whose son or daughter has enlisted for active military duty.

The truth is, no draft can ever be fair. Other than delighting America's hawks, the same favoritism and deference to influence and wealth—the well-documented kind George W. Bush probably received when he was granted a hard-to-get slot in the Texas Air National Guard because of his father's influence—will certainly prevail in any future draft. Anyone with political pull and family connections will always be able to avoid active military duty, or if not, receive plum, safe jobs.

Alienating Already-Cynical Youths

All a draft can do is help transform yet another generation of Americans . . . into potential cannon fodder. It also contributes to the further militarization of this country. "How many men and women," rightly asked Father Andrew Greeley, the *Chicago Sun-Times* columnist, "will be required to pacify Iraq and turn it into a freedom-loving democracy? How long will it take, how many lives must be sacrificed" . . . ?

The Draft Will Make Americans Turn Against Their Country

Since World War I the world has experienced continuous bloodletting, almost always enhanced by conscription. The Korean and Vietnam wars were both sustained because of the continual supply of new draftees, at least until the system broke down in the late Sixties when it became clear to our centrist elites that the United States had been defeated at a cost of 58,000 GI lives, hundreds of

Countries with No Draft

Antigua and Barbuda	Gambia	Malta	Sierra Leone
Australia	Ghana	Mauritania	South Africa
Bahamas	Grenada	Mauritius	Sri Lanka
Bahrain	Haiti	Monaco	Suriname
Bangladesh	Hong Kong	Myanmar	Swaziland
Barbados	Iceland	Nepal	Tonga
Belgium	India	Netherlands	Trinidad and Tobago
Belize	Ireland	New Zealand	Uganda
Botswana	Jamaica	Nicaragua	United Arab Emirates
Brunei Darussalam	Japan	Nigeria	United Kingdom of Great Britain
Burkina Faso	Jordan	Oman	and Northern Ireland
Burundi	Kenya	Pakistan	United States of America
Cameroon	Kyrgyzstan	Panama	Uruguay
Canada	Lesotho	Papua New Guinea	Vanuatu
Costa Rica	Luxembourg	Qatar	Zambia
Djibouti	Malawi	Rwanda	Zimbabwe
Fiji	Malaysia	San Marino	
Gabon	Maldives	Saudi Arabia	

Source: Office of the United Nations High Commissioner for Human Rights, 2001.

Some argue that drafting inexperienced and unskilled civilians into the army would only increase the toll of soldiers killed in war.

thousands of others wounded in body and mind and some 3 million Vietnamese—mainly civilians—dead.

And who bore the brunt of our recent wars? Draftees did.

The two world wars, Korea and Vietnam were largely fought with drafted soldiers who were killed or wounded in combat in far greater numbers than better-trained regulars. The lesson is clear: The more potential cannon fodder Selective Service can impress into the military, the more savage the war becomes, the longer it goes on and the greater the number of casualties. Another draft will allow policymakers to rely even more on war rather than diplomacy. It would certainly mean more military adventures abroad, more military and civilian deaths and ultimately more unrest at home.

Many pro-draft politicians are doubtless waiting for the [time] when a "safe" effort will be made to reintroduce conscription under the guise of fighting terrorism. For far too many, another draft means recapturing the mythical ethos of WWII—the "Good War"—and the pre-Sixties, when no one cared enough to protest governmental policies. In this imaginary Eden, there was no racial or religious conflict, women knew their place, support for tyrants abroad was justified in the name of fighting Communism, and young men called to the colors went willingly and patriotically to proudly serve their God and country. But please note that today many if not most pro-draft people in Congress and the White House are non-veterans.

A woman demonstrates on behalf of soldiers killed in Iraq. A draft would be unpopular with those who oppose war on the grounds that American lives should rarely be risked.

[In the spring of 2004] an article appeared in the *Baltimore Sun,* written by Nick Leonhardt, a high school senior. In it, he wrote:

Some anxious teens and their parents feel relieved that both President Bush and Senator John Kerry deny plans to reinstate the draft. But cynical youths already believe that candidates routinely break promises after they are elected. The man who shakes their hands during the presidential campaign may demand salutes after his inauguration.

Americans and especially its young should oppose conscription because it is a form of slavery and tramples on our freedom, which should never be sacrificed for ideological pipedreams and political manipulation.

Another draft is a terrible idea in a very troubled time.

EVALUATING THE AUTHOR'S ARGUMENTS:

Polner believes that the children of influential people will always be able to find ways to avoid military service. Based on what you have read in this viewpoint, do you think he has adequately supported his conclusions? Explain your answer.

A Draft Will Militarize Society

Katha Pollitt

"Conscription will make the country more authoritarian and probably more violent, too."

In the following viewpoint, Katha Pollitt argues that reinstating compulsory military service would be an ill-conceived and ill-timed move. She contends that it would actually militarize the country, and any perceived benefits would be outweighed by the cost to society: A more militarized nation, for example, would ultimately have to divert even more money to defense budgets. With a larger military force, Pollitt maintains, there would also be a greater likelihood of questionable military actions.

Katha Pollitt is an essayist, poet, and long-time columnist for the *Nation*.

AS YOU READ, CONSIDER THE FOLLOWING QUESTIONS:

1. Why does the author think that reinstating the draft would not lead to a stronger national commitment to unified sacrifice?
2. How does Pollitt answer claims that bringing back the draft could help strengthen antiwar sentiment?
3. What does the author suggest would be the economic consequences of a renewed draft?

S hould the government bring back the draft? Republican Senator Chuck Hagel has been talking it up, and it has captured the imagination of many liberals and leftists as well. [In 2003] antiwar Representative Charles Rangel of New York and Senator Fritz Hollings of South Carolina introduced proposals to restore the draft as a way to build opposition to the war: The draft, Rangel argued, would spread

Antiwar activists, such as these protesters outside a U.S. Marine Corps recruiting station, believe that recruiters unfairly lure America's youth into the military.

the burden of war throughout society and force war supporters in the upper classes to put their children where their mouths are.

The Draft Is a Bad Idea

On paper, it's a tempting argument. Universal conscription would certainly be a poke in the eye for [George] Bush, [Dick] Cheney, [Paul] Wolfowitz, [Douglas] Feith, [Richard] Perle and other prowar "chickenhawks" who used their social privilege to avoid Vietnam ("I had other priorities," said the Vice President, who enjoyed no fewer than five deferments). In theory, the draft would give us an army of "citizen soldiers," young men—and probably women—drawn from all parts of society, instead of the current Army, which draws heavily on military families, poor people and—to judge by Charles Graner [convicted of prisoner abuse in the Abu Ghraib scandal in Iraq], accepted into the Army in his early 30s despite a long history of violence and instability—wife-beating losers. For many, the draft summons up ideals of valor, adulthood, public service and self-sacrifice—shared self-sacrifice. Those are all good things, but the draft is still a bad idea.

Given our ever more stratified and atomized society, why expect the draft to be equal or fair? In the 1960s, the draft was famously open to evasion and manipulation, as that large flock of chickenhawks proves. The new draft would be too. The Army doesn't need every high school graduate—there are 612,836 men 18 to 26 in the Selective Service registry for the state of Ohio alone, more than four times the number of U.S. soldiers in Iraq—so it will be able, as in the past, to pick and choose. When one loophole closes, another will open: If Rangel succeeds in banning student deferments, we'll see 4Fs for college-bound kids with "attention deficit disorder" or "learning disabilities." Privileged kids will be funneled into safe stateside units, just the way George W. Bush was.

The Wrong Road to Awareness and Success

What about the argument that the draft will produce opposition to war? ("Parents and children would suddenly care," as historian of the 1960s Jon Wiener told me.) It's true that the draft will make it harder for kids and their families to live in a golden bubble—in the 1960s, the draft concentrated the minds of college students wonderfully well.

Mike Keefe. Copyright © 2003 by Mike Keefe. Reproduced by permission of Cagle Cartoons, Inc.

But mostly what the Vietnam-era draft produced was the abolition of the draft: That was the immediate form that opposition to the war took for those who most risked having to fight it. Abolishing the draft was a tremendous victory for the antiwar movement. If draftees were used in an unpopular war tomorrow, wouldn't opponents demand that kids not be forced to kill and be killed in an unjust and point-less cause? Nor is it entirely clear that a draft would raise antiwar sentiment overall. Conscription might make it harder, not easier, for many people to see a war's wrongness: It's hard to admit your children died in vain.

Supporters of the draft are using it to promote indirectly politics we should champion openly and up front. It's terrible that working-class teenagers join the Army to get college funds, or job training, or work—what kind of nation is this where [Iraq War soldiers] Jessica Lynch had to invade Iraq in order to fulfill her modest dream of becoming an elementary school teacher and Shoshanna Johnson had to be a cook on the battlefield to qualify for a culinary job back home? But the solution isn't to force more people into the Army, it's affordable education and good jobs for all. Nobody should have to choose between risking her life—or as we see in Abu Ghraib, her soul—and stocking shelves at Wal-Mart. By the same token, threatening our young with injury, madness and death is a rather roundabout way to increase resistance to military adventures. I'd rather just loudly insist that people who favor war go fight in it themselves or be damned as weasels and shirkers. . . .

A Militarized Nation

The main effect of bringing back the draft would be to further militarize the nation. The military has already thrust its tentacles deep into civilian life: We have ROTC [Reserve Officers' Training Corps] on campus, Junior ROTC in the high schools, Hummers in our garages and camouflage couture in our closets. Whole counties, entire professions, live or die by defense contracts—which is perhaps one reason we spend more on our military budget than the next twenty-five countries combined. (Did you know that the money raised by the breast

Some accuse the Reserve Officers' Training Corps (ROTC) program, which involves high school students such as these, of militarizing young people.

cancer postage stamp goes to the Defense Department?) Conscription will make the country more authoritarian and probably more violent, too, if that's possible—especially for women soldiers, who are raped and assaulted in great numbers in today's armed forces, usually with more or less impunity.

If we want a society that is equal, cohesive, fair and war-resistant, let's fight for that, not punish our children for what we have allowed America to become.

EVALUATING THE AUTHORS' ARGUMENTS:

In this viewpoint, Pollitt argues that a draft will make society more likely to justify and wage war, not make military service more equitable. Charles Moskos argues in the following viewpoint that a draft can make society more charitable and will restore a sense of national pride and civic duty in today's youth. After reading both viewpoints, which argument do you find more convincing? Why?

A Draft Can Make Society More Charitable

Charles Moskos

"A compulsory national service program would give our youth—and future leaders—a shaping civic experience."

Sociologist Charles Moskos argues in the following article that reinstating the draft is the only certain way for the United States to meet its security needs. Moskos explains that the ideal draft would include several tiers of service, beginning with eighteen-month tours of military duty for those aged eighteen to twenty-five. Other tiers could include service in homeland security agencies and groups such as the Peace Corps. By bringing back the draft and tying it to organizations other than the uniformed armed services, Moskos contends that the government would help spur an interest in public service among young people.

Charles Moskos is professor emeritus of sociology at Northwestern University in Evanston, Illinois.

AS YOU READ, CONSIDER THE FOLLOWING QUESTIONS:
1. Why does the author think that having a three-tiered draft would be more effective than a traditional draft program?

Charles Moskos, "Feel That Draft?" *Chicago Tribune,* June 8, 2005, p. 23. Copyright © 2005 by the *Chicago Tribune.* Reproduced by permission of the author.

2. How does Moskos respond to the claim that eighteen months is not long enough for military duty?

3. According to the author, what will be the result for the armed forces if the government does not create a new draft program?

Recruitment for the U.S. Army and Marine Corps is on the brink of disaster. Indeed, along with combat, recruiting duty is now considered the worst mission in the military. Although we are in a global war against terrorism, the American citizenry is not being asked for any sacrifice. In the last election, both President George W. Bush and Senator John Kerry (D-Mass.) were united in their refusal to consider a return to conscription. "Patriotism-lite" is the order of the day.

Reviving a Culture of Service

But truth to tell, a draft for the twenty-first century is the only answer to our national security needs. Such a draft would have three tiers of youth service, with eighteen-month tours of duty for citizens ages eighteen to twenty-five. The first tier would be modeled after a standard military draft. The second tier would be for homeland security, such as guarding our borders, ports, nuclear installations and chemical plants. Included in this category would be police officers, firefighters, air marshals and disaster medical technicians. The third tier would be for civilian national service, such as the Peace Corps, AmeriCorps, Habitat for Humanity, Teach for America, assistance for the elderly and infirm, environmental work and the like. Women should be draft-eligible for the latter two categories and, of course, can volunteer for military service as now.

In return, all draftees, as well as voluntary servers, would receive generous financial aid for college and graduate school modeled after the GI Bill of World War II. Non-servers would be ineligible for federal student aid. Today more than $20 billion annually in federal funds is given to students who do not serve their country. We have created a GI Bill of Rights without the "GI."

Any conscription system must start at the top of the social ladder to have widespread public acceptance. During World War II and the

Cold War, privileged youths were conscripted at a higher rate than youths from the lower socio-economic levels. (My draftee contemporary was Elvis Presley!) This was not true in the Vietnam War draft or in today's all-volunteer force. That only a handful of those in Congress have children in the military speaks directly to the inequity of military service today.

The Advantages of the Draft

Three major arguments are raised against conscription. These are given below with rejoinders.

1. Short enlistments would increase demands on the training base. Let us remember that almost one-third of our service entrants now fail to complete their initial enlistments. This contrasts with a 10 percent

AmeriCorps workers help in the aftermath of Hurricane Katrina. Some argue that a draft could motivate young people to serve their country at home.

In addition to providing young people with valuable skills, some believe a draft could provide Americans with a sense of purpose and belonging to their country.

dropout rate for draftees in the Cold War. Completion of an enlistment term is strongly correlated with higher education. It's much better to have a soldier serve a short draft tour honorably than be prematurely discharged. Conscription would both reduce personnel turnover and counter shortfalls in end strength.

2. The modern military requires highly technical skills that cannot be met by short-termers. Precisely. Higher compensation should be aimed at those whose skills require extended training and experience. In the draft era, the pay ratio between a senior non-commissioned officer and a private was six to one; today it is three to one. We now have overpaid recruits and underpaid sergeants.

3. Volunteers make better soldiers than those who are conscripted to serve. Item: in World War II, the Korean War and the Vietnam War, draftees had lower desertion and AWOL rates than volunteers. Item: Surveys of veterans find that draftees have a more favorable opinion of their military experience than do volunteers.

In brief, draftees could readily fill the multitude of jobs that require only a short formal training period or even just on-the-job training.

A marine takes pride in improving the lives of Iraqi children.

It is well documented that higher-quality recruits have the skills and motivation to learn quickly a wide variety of military jobs. Draftees would be ideally suited for duties on peacekeeping missions such as in Bosnia, Kosovo and the Sinai. Better educated and more mature draftees would also be ideal for guard duty in military prisons.

Enriching Our Civic Experience

Without conscription, what will happen? We will see, as is already happening, a lowering of military entrance standards. And, as is already occurring, there will be an exponential increase in enlistment bonuses. And we can expect new policies to recruit non-Americans into our armed forces, though we will probably call such a force a Freedom Legion rather than a Foreign Legion.

There is also a financial argument for conscription. Recruits in the all-volunteer force are three times more costly—in constant dollars—than draftees. The erosion of the citizen soldier has made for a career force that's top-heavy. The Pentagon now owes its soldiers $654 billion in future retirement benefits that it cannot pay.

Above all, a compulsory national service program would give our youth—and future leaders—a shaping civic experience. The revival of the citizen soldier can only be to the advantage of the armed services and the nation.

> ## EVALUATING THE AUTHOR'S ARGUMENTS:
>
> Moskos discusses the revival of the "citizen soldier" in this viewpoint, noting that a mandatory call to service will restore a sense of civic duty that has long been absent in the United States. Do you agree that today's young people lack the same commitment to civic duty that their parents or grandparents had? Why?

Chapter 3

Who Should Be Drafted?

Female soldiers participate in a training program. Whether it is appropriate to draft women and other groups into the army is a point of debate.

Viewpoint

1

Women Can Serve as Effectively as Men

Lory Manning

> *"Any discourse on women and war must acknowledge and discuss women as warriors."*

Lory Manning is a retired navy captain and currently director of the Women in the Military Project at the Women's Research and Education Institute in Washington, D.C. In the following viewpoint, Manning argues that women have served with distinction and bravery in the U.S. military since the Civil War and have proven themselves to be equal to the challenge of armed service. She objects to the policy that bars women from ground combat duty, which effectively prevents them from being able to rise to the top leadership positions. She contends that women who can withstand the physical rigors of the military should be afforded the same opportunities as men—and the same obligations, including the draft.

AS YOU READ, CONSIDER THE FOLLOWING QUESTIONS:
1. According to Manning, what percentage of U.S. soldiers serving in Iraq are women?

2. In the author's opinion, how does the United States compare with other nations that enlist women in their armed forces?
3. Why does the author argue in favor of allowing women to serve in dangerous battle situations?

Quick, which employer in the United States can—indeed must—discriminate against its employees based solely on their gender, without regard for their actual skills and talents? If you answered the U.S. military, you are right. This legal discrimination works against both sexes. Only men are required to register for the draft, and only women are prohibited from serving in the infantry, armor (such as tanks), most field artillery, special forces, and aboard submarines. War is, and has always been, a gendered pursuit. If you were a warrior, you were male; often, if you were male, you were a warrior. That logic is now coming apart in the United States and scores of other countries. Women today serve in the military forces of many nations, and they are no longer limited to supporting roles. Any discourse on women and war must acknowledge and discuss women as warriors, which means knowing something about who military women are, what they do, and how their roles have evolved.

Women Have Made Astounding Inroads

On September 30, 2003, according to the Defense Manpower Data Center (DMDC), there were 213,059 women (15 percent of the force) serving on active duty in the four Department of Defense services; 4,126 women serving in the active Coast Guard (10.7 percent)—part of the Department of Homeland Security; and 151,441 women (17.2 percent of the force) serving in the guard and reserve. Women are also entering the military at growing rates. According to DMDC, in fiscal year 2002, 18 percent of new army enlistees were women, as were 17 percent of the navy's, 7 percent of the marine corps' and 23 percent of the air force's. On the officer side, these percentages were 19 percent, 18 percent, 9 percent, and 23 percent, respectively. . . .

Women serve in every enlisted rank and in every officer rank except the four-star level—the highest rank now attainable—and chances are good that a woman will reach that rank within the next ten years.

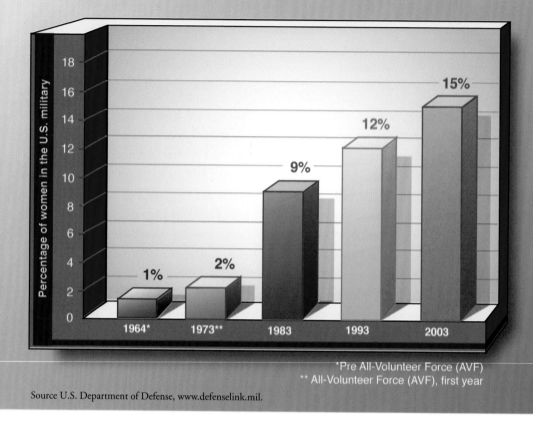

The U.S. Military Continues to Add Women

Percentage of women in the U.S. military

- 1964*: 1%
- 1973**: 2%
- 1983: 9%
- 1993: 12%
- 2003: 15%

*Pre All-Volunteer Force (AVF)
** All-Volunteer Force (AVF), first year

Source U.S. Department of Defense, www.defenselink.mil.

Women serve aboard—indeed, command—navy and coast guard ships, fly every sort of military aircraft, and serve in deployed army and marine corps units around the world. Over 10 percent of those serving in the current operations in Iraq are women.

Many who read these statistics will be astounded at the inroads women have quietly made into the supposedly males-only turf of the modern military in just over a century. The change began with a need for skilled nurses in both the Civil and Spanish-American Wars. . . . The navy established its own nurse corps in 1908. The next key change—the movement of women into military jobs other than nursing—came during World War I. The navy and marine corps brought women—including a few African-American women—onto active duty to serve as typists, telephone operators, and translators. These women were released from active duty as soon as the war ended, but their use during wartime set a precedent that was built upon during

World War II. Over 400,000 women served in that war in a wide range of military occupations, including gunnery instructors and mechanics. . . . The dedication and professional competence of these women convinced many military men, including Generals Eisenhower and Marshall, that the United States ought to keep a cadre of women on active duty in fields other than nursing after the war.

A Patriarchal History in the Military

This was accomplished through the passage of the Women's Armed Services Integration Act of 1948. People reading this legislation today will find it at best quaint and at worst downright patriarchal. They may wonder why any woman would choose to serve under its provisions. Yet for its time, it was radical. . . .

On the down side, the legislation limited women to no more than 2 percent of the total force and stipulated that women officers could be no more than 10 percent of that 2 percent. It capped women officers' rank at lieutenant colonel/commander, although one woman in each service could hold the temporary rank of colonel/captain while serving as head of its women's branch. It precluded husbands from receiving healthcare benefits, family housing, and access to military commissary and exchange facilities unless they were dependent on their wives for over 50 percent of their support, and it prohibited women from serving aboard navy ships—except hospital and transport ships—and aboard any aircraft that could have a combat mission. Women who became pregnant or who even lived in a household in which a child under 18 was present for more than 30 days per year were required to leave the service. Women were also forbidden by service policy from having command authority over men. This meant that while women could have men working for them, they could not award nonjudicial punishment to men or order them to court-martial. Without this authority, women were effectively barred from commanding any military unit or facility in which men served. . . .

> **FAST FACT**
>
> In 1948 President Harry S. Truman signed the Women's Armed Services Integration Act, which allowed women into the regular army and the Organized Reserve Corps.

Female marines learn how to use a gun in World War II. Women's role in the military has increased since the Women's Armed Services Integration Act was passed in 1948.

Notable Achievements

Over the next 50 years, the limitations placed on women's service by the 1948 law were toppled one by one through actions of the courts, Congress, and the services themselves. In 1967, Congress removed the caps on women's numbers and ranks, clearing the way for women admirals and generals and, incidentally, for the end of male conscription. Since then, women's rate of participation has gradually grown from less than two percent to today's 15 percent and climbing. In 1972, the Supreme Court decision in *Frontiero v. Richardson* awarded the husbands of military women the same benefits as the wives of military men. A U.S. Court of Appeals decision in the 1976 case *Crawford v. Cushman* found that regulations mandating the discharge of pregnant women violated their Fifth Amendment rights. That same year, Congress opened the service academies to women. During the

1970s, each of the services rewrote its policies so that women could award nonjudicial punishment and court-martial to men, thereby opening the way for women to command military units. The remaining two provisions of the 1948 law—the ban against women serving in aircraft with combat missions and aboard combat ships—were repealed by Congress in 1991 and 1994, respectively. Also in 1994, many previously closed army and marine corps units and positions were opened to women. Service assignment policies—which now require congressional notification before changes can be made—still bar U.S. servicewomen from serving in ground combat units. . . .

The Military Should No Longer Discriminate Against Women

[The] opening of combat arms to women [is] important because national-level military leaders are drawn only from the combat arms

Female soldiers compose 15 percent of the Department of Defense's total active duty force.

branches in most countries, and these military leaders play a critical role in national and international decision-making on strategy, operations, and fiscal appropriations. It's conceivable that the United States will have a woman member of the Joint Chiefs of Staff within the next decade or so. Women could also reach this level of influence in other countries where they serve in air, sea, or land combat, such as in most NATO [North Atlantic Treaty Organization] countries, Australia, New Zealand, South Africa, India, South Korea, Singapore, Brazil, Israel, and Japan. Women have served as heads of state, heads of government, defense ministers, and in every sort of cabinet post and legislative office. They are judges, professional athletes, and bishops. They run NGOs [nongovernmental organizations], universities, and multinational corporations, but throughout modern history right up to today, not one woman has been a national-level military commander. Soon that will change. Our thinking about women and war must expand to encompass this change.

EVALUATING THE AUTHOR'S ARGUMENTS:

In this viewpoint, Manning provides historical background on the role of women in the military. In what way does this information strengthen her arguments for increasing opportunities for women in the military? Explain your response.

Women Are Not as Effective as Men in Combat

Phyllis Schlafly

"Denial of physical differences is an illusion that kills."

In the following viewpoint, Phyllis Schlafly argues that allowing women into combat will be disastrous because women, no matter how brave, are not physically as strong as men and cannot readily carry extra military gear or a wounded fellow soldier. The push for women in combat, she contends, is nothing more than part of a feminist agenda that refuses to recognize any differences, even biological ones, between women and men. She adds that countries that have attempted to place women in combat have found those differences insurmountable.

Phyllis Schlafly, a lawyer, is a leading figure in the conservative political movement and a longtime critic of the feminist movement.

AS YOU READ, CONSIDER THE FOLLOWING QUESTIONS:

1. In what way has the military been vague about its stand on women's role in the military, according to Schlafly?

Phyllis Schlafly, "Women Don't Belong in Ground Combat," Eagle Forum, www.eagleforum.org, June 1, 2005. Reproduced by permission of the author.

2. What does the author believe would be the result of putting women in ground combat?
3. How many women have been killed and wounded in the Iraq war, as reported by the author?

W hy are our generals trying to push women into ground combat in Iraq despite Pentagon regulations and congressional law against it? What is it about civilian control of the military that the generals don't understand?

Women Do Not Belong in Ground Combat

Current Department of Defense [DoD] regulations exclude women from ground combat, as well as from assignment to forward support units that "collocate [i.e., are embedded side by side] with units assigned a direct ground combat mission." Federal law requires that Congress be given thirty legislative days' advance notice of any change to this policy.

Army Secretary Francis Harvey has been skirting (pardon the word) this policy by unilaterally rewording it to assign women to forward-support units except when "*conducting* an assigned direct ground combat mission." (emphasis added) When a ground-combat unit actually engages the enemy, the women (who are slated to be roughly 10 percent of the forward-support companies) will have to be evacuated from the battlefield.

How many ground and air vehicles, and how many extra men, will this ridiculous plan require? Will the enemy hold his fire until the evacuation is complete?

Frustrated by the Army's devious behavior, Reps. Duncan Hunter (R-CA) and John McHugh (R-NY) tried to add an amendment to the military appropriations bill to codify the current DoD regulations which the Army seems to have difficulty understanding. The feminists are lining up their media allies to demand that women be forced into land combat situations, while falsely asserting that Hunter-McHugh is "changing" the rule.

Majority of Women Oppose Combat Assignments

Much of the demand for women in combat comes from female officers who are eager for medals and promotions. Enlisted women are acutely aware of the heavy lifting that must be done by the combat infantry.

The Army's own opinion surveys prior to 2001 consistently reported that 85 to 90 percent of enlisted women oppose "being assigned to combat units on the same basis as men." Women enlistees have a right to expect the Army to obey current policy and law.

The advocates of women in combat say the front line is everywhere in Iraq. They continually try to fuzzy over the difference between being subject to risk (such as being ambushed by a car bomb) versus the task of aggressively seeking out and killing the enemy.

Army Chief of Staff General Peter J. Schoomaker tried to laugh off the difference by saying that "maybe since we're killing 40,000 people a year on the highways, they [women] shouldn't drive. That's very

Female soldiers participate in a training exercise. To what extent women should participate in combat is hotly debated.

dangerous, too." Comparing the risk of highway driving with engaging the enemy in combat is insulting to our intelligence and common sense.

Putting women in military combat is the cutting edge of the feminist goal to force us into an androgynous society. Feminists are determined to impose what Gloria Steinem called "liberation biology" that pretends all male-female differences are culturally imposed by a discriminatory patriarchy.

History offers no evidence for the proposition that the assignment of women to military combat jobs is the way to win wars, improve combat readiness, or promote national security.

Physical Differences Are Real and Critical

Women, on the average, have only 60 percent of the physical strength of men, are about six inches shorter, and survive basic training only

A female airman dresses her son. Assigning females to combat is opposed by those who believe it would take mothers away from their children.

U.S. Army honor guards carry the coffin of Sgt. Myla Maravillosa, the first Filipino American woman killed in Iraq.

by the subterfuge of being graded on effort rather than on perform-ance. These facts, self-evident to anyone who watches professional or Olympic sports competitions, are only some of the many sex differ-ences confirmed by scholarly studies.

Denial of physical differences is an illusion that kills. That's the les-son of the Atlanta courtroom massacre where a 5-foot-1, 51-year-old grandmother police guard was overpowered by a 6-foot-tall, 210-pound former football linebacker criminal; so now three people are dead.

Every country that has experimented with women in actual com-bat has abandoned the idea, and the notion that Israel uses women in combat is a feminist myth. The armies and navies of every poten-tial enemy are exclusively male; their combat readiness is not dimin-ished by coed complications or social experimentation.

The 1992 Presidential Commission on the Assignment of Women in the Armed Forces voted to maintain the exemption of women from assignment to combat in ground troops, combat aviation, amphibi-ous ships and submarines. But already thirty-three servicewomen includ-ing mothers have been killed and 270 wounded in the war in Iraq.

Do Not Send Mothers to War

The Army is wondering why it can't meet its recruitment goals. It could be that the current 15 percent female quota is a turn-off to men who don't want to fight alongside of women who can't carry a man off the battlefield if he is wounded. Forcing women in or near land combat will hurt recruiting, not help.

No country in history ever sent mothers of toddlers off to fight enemy soldiers until the United States did this in the Iraq war. We hope this won't be the legacy of the Bush Administration.

EVALUATING THE AUTHORS' ARGUMENTS:

Schlafly argues in this viewpoint that women should be kept from ground combat because they are not physically as strong as men. Lory Manning, the author of the previous viewpoint, believes women can do as good a job as men in combat. After reading both viewpoints, do you feel women should remain exempt from actual combat duty or that they should serve alongside men? Why?

The Military Targets Minorities for Service

"It is unlikely that many Latinos will be filling the Pentagon's civilian or policy-making positions in the coming decades. . . . Latino youth will be shipping out to fight foreign wars."

Arlene Inouye and Jorge Mariscal

In the following viewpoint, Arlene Inouye and Jorge Mariscal argue that military recruiters focus on enlisting minorities rather than seeking a broad base of recruits. They charge recruiters with focusing on Latino high school students, many of whom come from poor neighborhoods and have limited opportunities for higher education or employment training. According to Inouye and Mariscal, recruiters make military service sound appealing but do not fully disclose the realities of serving during wartime—which gives students an inaccurate view of service.

Arlene Inouye is founder and coordinator of the Coalition Against Militarism in the Schools (CAMS). Jorge Mariscal, professor of Spanish and Chicano literature at the University of California, San Diego, is active in groups opposing school-based military recruitment.

Arlene Inouye and Jorge Mariscal, "Hispanic Heritage Month Means Covert Recruiting," *Draft Notices,* November/December 2005. Reproduced by permission of the publisher and the authors.

AS YOU READ, CONSIDER THE FOLLOWING QUESTIONS:
1. According to the authors, how do military recruiters tie their efforts to school events?
2. What are the key selling points recruiters make when talking to students about service?
3. What four regions were visited by the "Medal of Honor Tour," and what conclusion do the authors draw from this information?

On October 7, 2005, at the Anaheim, California, Convention Center not far from Disneyland, the Hispanic Engineer National Achievement Corporation hosted an awards luncheon for approximately 500 people including more than 300 middle school, high school and college students. The featured employer at the luncheon was the Department of Defense.

Trying to Attract Minorities

Part of the Pentagon's ongoing efforts to attract more Latinos into its ranks, the luncheon included Latino ROTC [Reserve Officers' Training Corps] and military service academy students and a display that forms part of the "Medal of Honor Tour," a joint venture between the Army and the Hispanic public relations agency Cartel Impacto (a unit of The Cartel Group of San Antonio, Texas). According to the official press release, the tour is a "national program to highlight the selfless and courageous legacy of service Hispanic Americans have imprinted in our nation's armed services."

One day earlier, the "Medal of Honor Tour" had descended upon Roosevelt High School in East Los Angeles. Accompanied by a JROTC [Junior ROTC] color guard, the display was presented to students by Rick Leal, President of the Medal of Honor Society. Leal's remarks were followed by presentations by City Councilman Tony Cardenas and Ramon Rodriguez, a local veteran who served three tours in Vietnam.

Elaborate Plans to Recruit Latinos

Rodriguez's remarks were the stuff of a recruiter's fantasy. He stated that although he had almost dropped out of high school, he ended up earning three advanced degrees "all because of the military." He repeatedly stated that he owed a great deal to the military, highlighted career and education benefits, and urged students to join JROTC. He concluded by saying: "Freedom is not free, it has to be fought for."

It will surprise no one who has followed the Pentagon's elaborate plans to recruit Latino youth that the four regions chosen to host the "Medal of Honor Tour" are Phoenix, San Antonio, L.A./Anaheim, and San Jose/San Francisco. The U.S. Army Recruiting Command's Strategic Initiative, 2002–2007, designates each of these locations as among the primary markets for the recruitment of Latino youth.

Selling a Pretty Picture

After the presentation at Roosevelt, we spoke to a young Latina senior who had received a call from a recruiter the week before the "Medal

Students protest military recruitment efforts on the grounds that they disproportionately target minority communities.

of Honor Tour" had appeared at her school. The recruiter told her that women were not sent into combat and she would not have to fight (as of the end of October [2005], forty-seven U.S. servicewomen had died in Iraq). He added that she most likely would enjoy Iraq because many of the bases there had swimming pools and basketball courts.

In Anaheim, on the day after the event in East Los Angeles, the Pentagon spokesman directly addressed teachers and counselors by noting that there were "some key influencers of our society" in the audience. "I call on you to help increase the representation of Hispanics in the Department of Defense," he said, "by telling young people about the opportunities and value of service to our country either in the military ranks or as civil servants.

"The military affords our young people the opportunity to gain responsibility fast and develop leadership skills that can't be obtained anywhere else, from leading a platoon in battle to flying an aircraft off the deck of an aircraft carrier in high seas to developing departmental policy," he said. In a concluding remark that sounded more

Jeff Parker. Copyright © 2005 by Jeff Parker. Reproduced by permission of Cagle Cartoons, Inc.

Critics of the draft argue that minorities, such as this Latina cadet, occupy the lowest ranks of the military where they experience the highest risk of being killed.

like an afterthought, he added: "And our civilian jobs offer exciting and rewarding career opportunities as well."

The Reality of Latinos in the Military

Given the shockingly low percentages of Latino youth in higher education and professional schools, it is unlikely that many Latinos will be filling the Pentagon's civilian or policy-making positions in the coming decades. Instead, because the current situation in which the vast majority of Latino men and women in the U.S. armed forces are bunched together in the lowest ranks is unlikely to change, Latino youth will be shipping out to fight foreign wars like the one in Iraq. Some of them will die there and they will be added to the list of names in some covert recruiting "Medal of Honor Tour" of the future.

EVALUATING THE AUTHORS' ARGUMENTS:

The authors argue that the drive to recruit Latino students for the military unfairly plays on stereotypes and fears that young Latinos have fewer opportunities than other groups. Based on your knowledge of the topic, do you think their comments could be used to argue in favor of conscription? Explain your answer.

The Military Does Not Target Minorities for Service

"The current makeup of the all-volunteer military looks like America."

Tim Kane

Tim Kane argues in the following viewpoint that Pentagon data indicate the military does not target minorities for recruitment. This excerpt from a detailed study claims that whites make up the bulk of soldiers, minorities serve proportionately, and that a draft would force more minorities into service. He concludes that the all-volunteer military force reflects the racial distribution in America.

Tim Kane is Bradley Research Fellow in Labor Policy at the Heritage Foundation's Center for Data Analysis.

AS YOU READ, CONSIDER THE FOLLOWING QUESTIONS:

1. According to the author, how do military recruits compare with the general population in level of education?
2. In Kane's opinion, does the military favor well-educated recruits who also happen to come from underprivileged neighborhoods?
3. Does the author believe that the military needs to revamp its recruitment policies, including reinstating a draft?

A few Members of Congress, motivated by American combat in the Middle East, have called for the reinstatement of a compulsory military draft. The case for coercing young citizens to join the military is supposedly based on social justice—that all should serve—and seems to be buttressed by reports of shortfalls in voluntary enlistment. In a *New York Times* op-ed on December 31, 2002, Representative Charles Rangel (D-NY) claimed, "A disproportionate number of the poor and members of minority groups make up the enlisted ranks of the military, while most privileged Americans are underrepresented or absent." This claim is frequently repeated by critics of the war in Iraq. Aside from the logical fallacy that a draft is less offensive to justice than a voluntary policy, Rangel's assertions about the demographic makeup of the enlisted military are not grounded in fact. . . .

Representative Rangel's theory is that if all citizens faced equal prospects of dying in a conflict, support for that conflict would have to pass a higher standard. This theory assumes that the privileged classes would be less willing to commit the nation to war if that conflict involved personal, familial, or class bloodshed. It also assumes that the existing volunteers are either ignorant or lack other options—that is, they are involuntary participants. One way to test this thesis is to explore the demographic patterns of enlisted recruits before and after the initiation of the global war on terrorism on September 11, 2001. . . .

> **FAST FACT**
>
> As of 2002, according to the U.S. Department of Defense, 83 percent of all officers in the U.S. military were white, while 64 percent of all enlisted men were white.

Proportional Racial Representation Among Recruits

We found that whites are one of the most proportionally represented groups—making up 77.4 percent of the population and 75.8 percent of all recruits—whereas other racial categories are often represented in noticeably higher and lower proportions than the general population.

This kind of racial analysis is complicated by the fact that race is a self-identified attribute that is not well defined genetically, and many citizens object to racial classification, which complicates government efforts to categorize racial and ethnic identity consistently. Specifically, race data for the population in 2000 are not compatible with the 1999 recruit cohort but are compatible with the 2003 cohort. The 1999 recruit data allow for only one race category per person, whereas 2003 recruit and Census data follow a system that both allows each individual to self-identify any combination of six racial categories and includes an independent Hispanic indicator.

A Draft Would Put More Minorities into Service

The following analysis of race is based on a comparison of the 2003 recruit data and Census population data for ages 18 and above (not just 18–24). . . . The data show that, proportionally, blacks make up

The Department of Defense claims that the racial breakdown of the military accurately reflects societal demographics.

43 percent more of the Army recruits than does the general population, but this is not in place of whites, who make up 1 percent more (not less). Other racial categories—notably American Indians/Alaskan Natives (53 percent) and Native Hawaiian/Pacific Islanders (249 percent)—are even more overrepresented.

A military draft along the lines proposed by Representative Rangel would press thousands more Asian-Americans into service, as well as thousands of Americans who decline to be racially categorized. In contrast, a draft could deny blacks, whites, and others the freedom to enlist in the Army once their racial quotas were filled.

Explaining the Numbers

We next considered the "underprivileged source" hypothesis. We know from earlier analysis that recruiting is not concentrated in poor neigh-

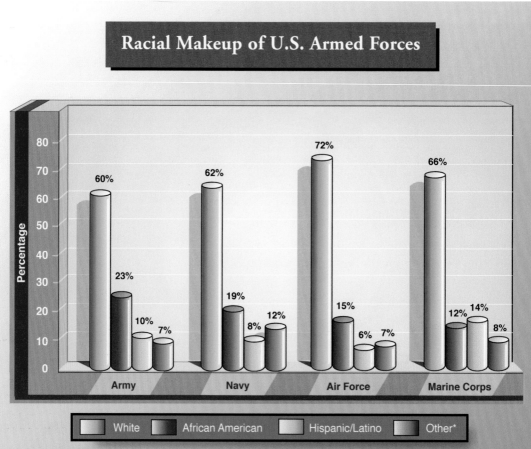

Racial Makeup of U.S. Armed Forces

*"Other" includes Asian American/Pacific Islander, American Indian/Alaskan Native, and Other/Unknown.
Note: Rows may not total 100 percent because of rounding.

Source: Government Accountability Office (GAO), analysis of U.S. Department of Defense data, www.gao.gov, March 2004.

African American soldiers are not more heavily recruited for service, argue military sources, but join because they, like other Americans, want to serve their country.

borhoods (ZCTAs), but perhaps it is disproportionately concentrated in black neighborhoods.

The 100 three-digit ZCTAs with the highest concentration of blacks (in any combination of other races) range from 24.05 percent up to 68.63 percent self-identified as black. These areas have 14.63 percent of the adult population but are the origin of only 16.58 percent of 1999 recruits and 14.09 percent of 2003 recruits. Moreover, 2003 recruits from these "black" areas included an almost equal number of white and black recruits (45.7 percent and 46 percent of the total, respectively). The group of ZCTAs with the highest concentration of whites had almost 46 times as many white recruits as black recruits. Among the ZCTAs that had the highest number of recruits, the ratio was almost 4:1. If the military were to draw disproportionately from minority groups by design, one would expect fewer white recruits from minority-concentrated areas and more minority recruits from the white-concentrated areas.

Minorities Not Heavily Recruited

The demographic data on race reveal that military enlistees are not, in fact, more heavily recruited from black neighborhoods. The data also reveal that minorities serve in different proportions, but not because fewer whites are serving. In other words, there is no "disproportionate share of minorities" serving in the military, as claimed by editorials around the nation in 2003. Some minorities participate more heavily than other minorities.

Race is often used as a proxy for class, but it is rarely, if ever, an appropriate substitute. Even if the military had a higher share of African-Americans, it does not follow that those recruits are poorer, from poorer areas, from more urbanized areas, less educated, or from less educated areas. Indeed, none of these other claims can be substantiated. . . .

The Military Looks Like America

Put simply, the current makeup of the all-voluntary military looks like America. Where they are different, the data show that the average soldier is slightly better educated and comes from a slightly wealthier, more rural area. We found that the military (and Army specifically) included a higher proportion of blacks and lower proportions of other minorities but a proportionate number of whites. More important, we found that recruiting was not drawing disproportionately from racially concentrated areas.

Perhaps more could be done to dismantle the claim that an all-volunteer military relies disproportionately on ignorant, black, poor, urban young citizens in America, but the evidence already clearly shows this claim to be hollow.

EVALUATING THE AUTHOR'S ARGUMENTS:

In this viewpoint, Tim Kane argues that the education level of recruits actually went up after the terrorist attacks of September 11, 2001. He believes that the quality of recruits has therefore actually gone up in the past few years. Based on his arguments and the data he presents, do you think he makes his case that reinstating the draft is not necessary? Why or why not?

Facts About the Military and the Draft

Editor's note: These facts can be used in reports or papers to reinforce or add credibility when making important points or claims.

Who Is Serving?
- As of September 2005, the Selective Service System had 13.5 million names of males aged eighteen to twenty-five on its registration rolls.
- According to the U.S. Department of Labor, 85 percent of the current personnel of the armed forces are enlisted, while 15 percent are officers.
- According to the U.S. Department of Defense, the breakdown of military personnel by race in 2002 for enlisted men was 64 percent white, 20 percent black, 10 percent Latino, and 6 percent Asian and other.
- For officers, the breakdown was 83 percent white, 9 percent black, 4 percent Latino, and 5 percent Asian and other.
- According to the Bureau of Labor Statistics, the average age of enlisted military recruits is 20.1 years.

Use of the Draft
- The U.S. Constitution does not specifically call for a draft, but it does authorize Congress to "raise and support Armies."
- The Confederacy began drafting men in April 1862, nearly a year before the Union instituted a draft.
- According to Mothers Against the Draft, until the twentieth century, males up to age forty-five could be called to serve in the military. Briefly in 1865, the Confederacy called up able-bodied fifty-year-olds.
- The first peacetime conscription was introduced in Prussia at the beginning of the nineteenth century.
- The Selective Service Act was passed by Congress during World War I; it established the Selective Service System and conscripted men aged twenty-one to thirty.
- According to the Selective Service System, the first peacetime draft in the United States was enacted in 1940, a year before the Japanese attacked Pearl Harbor.

- Selective Service figures show that during the twentieth century, the largest number of men (3.3 million) were drafted in 1943. The smallest number (646) was in 1973, the last year the draft was used.
- During the Korean Conflict (1950–1953), World War II veterans were exempt from the draft.

If the Draft Is Reinstated

According to the Selective Service System:

- In the event the draft is reinstated, college students could have their induction postponed until the end of the current semester. (Seniors would be allowed to finish their academic year.)
- Married men, or men with a dependent child, would not receive any special treatment. (In the past, a married man who was also a father could receive a "hardship to dependents" deferment.)
- A lottery based on birthdays would determine the order in which registered men are called for duty. The first to be called, in a sequence determined by the lottery, would be men whose 20th birthday falls during that year, followed, if needed, by 21- to 25-year-olds and then by 18- and 19-year-olds.

Women and the Military

- More than two thousand women volunteered as nurses (many serving on the battlefield) during the Civil War. One of the key figures in the volunteer effort was Clara Barton, who founded the American Red Cross in 1881.
- According to the Selective Service System, more than 150,000 women volunteered to serve during World War II. The Women's Army Auxiliary Corps (WAAC) was formed in 1941 to allow women to serve in clerical and support roles in the army.
- The Defense Manpower Data Center (DMDC) reports that as of 2004, 20.2 percent of all active applicants for military service were women.
- According to the U.S. Census Bureau, women make up 16 percent of veterans of the Persian Gulf War (1990–1991). In contrast, fewer than 5 percent of veterans from earlier wars were women.
- Women have never been drafted, even during wartime.
- Congress would have to amend the Selective Service law to add women to the draft.

Conscientious Objectors and Draft Resisters

- The first claim for conscientious objector status in America was in 1658; "conscientious objector" was officially recognized as a non-combatant category during the Civil War.
- According to Mothers Against the Draft, during the Civil War both Northern and Southern men who did not want to fight could hire "substitutes" to take their place in the draft for three hundred dollars.
- The Selective Service offers alternative service programs for those who are classified as conscientious objectors to military action for religious or moral reasons, but all males must register regardless of their beliefs.
- According to the Canadian Broadcasting Corporation, as many as 125,000 draft-aged men fled to Canada to avoid being drafted by the United States during the Vietnam War.
- According to federal law, failing to register with the Selective Service results in penalties of as much as $250,000, a prison term of up to five years, or both if tried and convicted.
- Mothers Against the Draft reports that the antiwar protests and riots of the 1960s against the Vietnam War were the first such riots in the United States since the Civil War.

Glossary

All-Volunteer Force (AVF): The current military force in the United States in which all troops are drawn from civilian volunteers rather than a compulsory service requirement. The U.S. Armed Forces has been an AVF since July 1973.

armed forces: The branches of the military, which in the United States consists of the army, navy, marines, air force, and coast guard.

civilian: One who is not a member of the military; a private citizen.

combat: In military terms, active engagement in fighting or defense. Combat can be conducted with weapons from large missiles to hand grenades and guns; it can also be hand-to-hand. In the United States military, women are not permitted to engage in active ground and naval combat, although they are allowed to engage in limited air combat.

compulsory service: Required service in the military, as during a draft. In some countries military service is required of all male citizens. In the United States, although in theory not every man is required to serve, during a draft all eligible men can be called at any time.

conscientious objector: One who refuses to fight for personal reasons, most often religious. Often, conscientious objectors will not serve even in a noncombatant role (see **noncombatant**). Conscientious objectors must apply for this status; it is not granted automatically.

conscription: The act of drafting a civilian into military service.

draft board: A civilian group charged with classifying, registering, and selecting conscripts. In the event of a draft, the Selective Service System would appoint volunteers to local boards within their communities.

draft dodger (or draft evader): One who evades the call to duty. During the Vietnam War, many draft dodgers fled to Canada.

draft lottery: The system by which draft numbers are chosen to determine who will be conscripted into the military. Discontinued in 1942 and reinstated in 1969 through 1973, the lottery is considered a more random and thus a fairer way to choose who will be conscripted first.

draft number: The number assigned to each eligible man in a lottery.

National Guard: The National Guard, the only branch of the military actually required under the U.S. Constitution, is made up of civilian volunteers who commit a portion of their time to training and readiness missions. Volunteers can join either the Army or Air National Guard. The National Guard is often called upon to assist in peacetime crises (such as natural disasters). During wartime, Guard members can be called up to serve as full-time soldiers.

noncombatant: One who does not engage in combat. This could be a civilian, a conscientious objector, or a serving member of the military (such as a chaplain) whose duties do not include combat.

registration: The process through which young men eligible for a potential draft provide the federal government with information that will allow the government to draft them. Registration ended in 1975 but was reinstated in 1980 by President Jimmy Carter as a safeguard against potential military action in light of the Soviet invasion of Afghanistan.

Selective Service System: The independent federal organization responsible for administering the draft during those times when a draft is in place. The Selective Service System is responsible for the draft registration process, which currently requires that all men between the ages of eighteen and twenty-six must register in the event of a possible draft.

Selective Training and Service Act: The law that established a peacetime draft in the United States for the first time and that established the Selective Service System as an independent federal agency. It was signed into law by President Franklin D. Roosevelt in anticipation of possible American involvement in World War II.

veteran: One who has served in the military, either during wartime or as part of a set tour of duty in peacetime.

Organizations to Contact

American Civil Liberties Union
125 Broad St., 18th Fl.
New York, NY 10004-2400
(800) 567-ACLU
Web site: www.aclu.org

The American Civil Liberties Union works to defend the rights and freedoms of individuals on a variety of issues, including the draft. The ACLU comes to the aid, for example, of those seeking conscientious objector status but who are nonetheless called to serve in battle.

Center for Military Readiness
PO Box 51600
Livonia, MI 48151
(202) 347-5333
e-mail: info@cmrlink.org
Web site: www.cmrlink.org

The Center for Military Readiness is an educational organization that focuses on issues concerning military personnel. It promotes high standards in military training and efficiency and believes the most important issue for the military is to deter aggression whenever possible and to protect the United States.

Center on Conscience and War (CCW)
1830 Connecticut Ave. NW
Washington, DC 20009
(202) 483-2220
(800) 379-2679
e-mail: ccw@centeronconscience.org
Web site: www.centeronconscience.org

The Center on Conscience and War is an association of religious bodies that work together to defend the rights of conscientious objectors. It is opposed to all types of military conscription.

Eagle Forum
PO Box 618
Alton, IL 62002
(618) 462-5415
e-mail: eagle@eagleforum.org
Web site: www.eagleforum.org

Founded by Phyllis Schlafly, best known as an opponent of the proposed Equal Rights Amendment, the Eagle Forum provides "pro-family" viewpoints on a variety of issues, including the military draft, in particular the question of whether women should be drafted or allowed to serve in combat with men.

Friends Committee on National Legislation (FCNL)
245 Second St. NE
Washington, DC 20002
(202) 547-6000
(800) 630-1330
Web site: www.fcnl.org

Founded during World War II by the Religious Society of Friends (Quakers), FCNL is the largest peace lobby in Washington, D.C. It played an instrumental role in the development of the Peace Corps in the early 1960s. In addition to a number of pamphlets and brochures, FCNL also publishes a monthly newsletter.

Mothers Against the Draft
PO Box 656
Sparks, NV 89432
(775) 356-9009
e-mail: info@mothersagainstthedraft.org
Web site: www.mothersagainstthedraft.org

Mothers Against the Draft was founded by a group of concerned mothers from across the political spectrum who oppose the reinstatement of compulsory military service. They believe that the U.S. military is dangerously overextended, and they oppose preemptive military actions that will of necessity increase the number of troops needed in combat. They also oppose drafting women and placing current women soldiers in combat.

560

Project for Youth and Non-military Opportunities (Project YANO)
PO Box 230157
Encinitas, CA 92023
(760) 634-3604
e-mail: projyano@aol.com
Web site: www.projectyano.org

Project YANO focuses on low-income and minority students and provides them with information about the military as well as alternatives to military enlistment. The founders of Project YANO believe that low-income and minority youths are disproportionately targeted for military recruitment, often with false expectations about what to expect from military service.

Selective Service System
National Headquarters
Arlington, VA 22209-2405
(703) 605-4100
e-mail: information@sss.gov
Web site: www.sss.gov

The Selective Service System, an independent federal agency, oversees conscription of eligible individuals to serve in the military in the event of a need for extra manpower (such as a declaration of war). It is also charged with finding alternative service programs for anyone classified as a conscientious objector. In addition to numerous surveys and reports for the U.S. government, the Selective Service also publishes a bimonthly newsletter, the *Register*.

U.S. Department of Defense
The Pentagon
Washington, DC 20301
Web site: www.dod.gov

Encompassing the army, navy, air force, marines, coast guard, and National Guard, the Department of Defense is the agency responsible for providing military forces and equipment to protect the United States from attack. It was created in 1949 by an act of Congress and is headquartered in the Pentagon, one of the most recognizable office complexes in the world. The Department of Defense oversees more than 3 million active duty and reserve troops.

U.S. Department of Homeland Security (DHS)

Washington, DC 20528
(202) 282-8010
Web site: www.dhs.gov

Created in response to the terrorist attacks on New York and Washington on September 11, 2001, the Department of Homeland Security united functions of the Departments of Justice, Treasury, Defense, Energy, Commerce, Agriculture, and Transportation under one umbrella. The goal of DHS is to streamline the operations of these diverse offices as a means of better protecting the United States from enemy attacks.

U.S. Department of Veterans Affairs

810 Vermont Ave. NW
Washington, DC 20420
(800) 827-1000
Web site: www.va.gov

The Department of Veterans Affairs, a cabinet-level agency since 1989, oversees such veterans issues as pensions, long-term care, insurance, burial, and survivor benefits. With origins dating back to 1636, the department serves 25 million living veterans and another 45 million spouses and dependents of veterans.

Veterans of Foreign Wars (VFW)

200 Maryland Ave. NE
Washington, DC 20002
(202) 543-2239
e-mail: vfw@vfwdc.org
Web site: www.vfw.org

With some 2.4 million members and nine thousand posts around the world, the VFW looks after the needs of those who have served in the U.S. armed forces. It has worked to improve benefits for veterans, such as medical care and fair compensation. The VFW also works to educate the public about the role the military plays in society and the importance of contributing to society by providing some sort of service.

For Further Reading

Books

Anderson, Martin, ed., with Barbara Honegger, *The Military Draft: Selected Readings on Conscription.* Stanford, CA: Hoover Institution, 1982. A selection of essays focusing on various aspects of conscription in the United States.

Chambers, John Whiteclay, *To Raise an Army.* New York: Free Press, 1987. An analysis of various forms of conscription in the U.S. from the American Revolution to the twentieth century and its political and social implications.

Cohen, Eliot A., *Citizens and Soldiers: The Dilemmas of Military Service.* Ithaca, NY: Cornell University Press, 1990. Examines the geopolitical considerations of raising an army in modern times.

Elmer, Jerry, *Felon for Peace: The Memoir of a Vietnam-Era Draft Resister.* Nashville, TN: Vanderbilt University Press, 2005. The author tells about his decision to resist the draft in the 1960s and the impact it had on his life.

Ensign, Tod, ed., *America's Military Today: The Challenge of American Militarism.* New York: W.W. Norton, 2004. A series of essays on current social and tactical issues facing American troops in the twenty-first century.

Fick, Nathaniel C., *One Bullet Away: The Making of a Marine Officer.* New York: Houghton Mifflin, 2005. A personal account of serving with the marines in Afghanistan and Iraq.

Flynn, George Q., *Conscription and Democracy: The Draft in France, Great Britain, and the United States.* Westport, CT: Greenwood, 2001. An analysis of conscription in three countries in times of war, examining each country's successes and challenges in creating a strong and effective military.

Gold, Philip, *The Coming Draft: The Crisis in Our Military and Why Selective Service Is Wrong for America.* New York: Presidio, 2006. Discusses why compulsory conscription is not the answer to solving today's military challenges.

Griffith, Robert K., *United States Army's Transition to the All-Volunteer Force, 1968–74.* Washington, DC: Department of the Army, 1997. Provides the army's perspective on the switch to an all-volunteer force in the 1970s.

Johnson, R. Charles, and Charles E. Sherman, *Draft Registration and the Law: A Guidebook.* Occidental, CA: Nolo, 1991. Provides useful information for young men approaching draft registration age.

Kohn, Stephen M., *Jailed for Peace: The History of American Draft Law Violators, 1658–1985.* Westport, CT: Greenwood, 1986. An exploration of draft evaders and conscientious objectors from colonial times to the post-Vietnam era.

Kusch, Frank, *All American Boys: Draft Dodgers in Canada from the Vietnam War.* Westport, CT: Praeger, 2001. Discusses the reasons young men went to Canada rather than serve in Vietnam.

Neiberg, Michael S., *Making Citizen-Soldiers: ROTC and the Ideology of American Military Service.* Cambridge, MA: Harvard University Press, 2001. Provides an overview and history of the Reserve Officers' Training Corps (ROTC) college recruitment program.

O'Hanlon, Michael E., *Defense Strategy for the Post-Saddam Era.* Washington, DC: Brookings Institution, 2005. An examination of strategic goals in light of American military experiences in the twenty-first century.

Roth-Douquet, Kathy, and Frank Schaeffer, *AWOL: The Unexcused Absence of America's Upper Classes from the Military—and How It Hurts Our Country.* New York: Collins, 2006. Explores the need for class integration in the armed forces and offers suggestions for more equitable service from all classes.

Segal, David R., *Recruiting for Uncle Sam: Citizenship and Military Manpower.* Lawrence: University Press of Kansas, 1992. A history and analysis of military recruitment and how modern needs can best be met.

Tracy, James, ed., *The Military Draft Handbook: A Brief History and Practical Advice for the Curious and Concerned.* San Francisco: Manic D, 2005. Provides comprehensive information about military recruitment, history of the draft, and the draft resistance movement throughout history.

Periodicals

Bandow, Doug, "Don't Wreck the Military with a Draft," *Conservative Chronicle,* October 13, 2004.

Barr, Bob, "Caught Up in the Draft," *UPI Perspectives,* November 2, 2004.

Congressional Digest, "Military Draft," May 2004.

Donnelly, Elaine, "Will Women Be Forced into Selective Service?" *Human Events,* August 15, 2005.

Donnelly, Thomas, "Force Size and Strategy," *National Security Outlook,* September 2004.

Ensign, Tod, "Draft Chatter," *Toward Freedom,* Fall 2004.

Gainza, Joseph, "Will There Be a Draft?" *Peacework,* November 2004.

Gonzales, Juan, "Racial Divide Evident in Military," *New York Daily News,* November 8, 2005.

Grigg, William Norman, "Get Ready for the Draft," *New American,* May 30, 2005.

Herbert, Bob, "War on the Cheap," *Liberal Opinion Week,* December 27, 2004.

Infield, Tom, "Peace-Churches Plan Alternatives to Military Draft," *Philadelphia Inquirer,* June 19, 2005.

Kagan, Frederick W., "The War Against Reserves," *National Security Outlook,* August 2005.

Kaplan, Fred, "Who's in the Army Now?" *Slate,* June 30, 2005.

Koehler, Robert C., "Counter-Recruiters: All the Charm of the Draft," *Human Quest,* July/August 2005.

Korb, Lawrence J., "All-Volunteer Army Shows Signs of Wear," *Atlanta Journal-Constitution,* February 27, 2005.

Lehman, John, "Diversity and the Draft," *Washington Post,* February 3, 2003.

Maier, Francis X., "Biting the Bullet," *Crisis,* January 2005.

Moskos, Charles, "A New Concept of the Citizen-Soldier," *Orbis,* Fall 2005.

O'Hanlon, Michael E., "Forget About Military Draft," *Japan Times,* January 29, 2003.

Oi, Walter, "The Virtue of an All-Volunteer Force," *Regulation,* Summer 2003.

Page, Clarence, "Burning the Draft Card," *Liberal Opinion Week,* October 18, 2004.

Pear, Robert, "U.S. Has Contingency Plans for Draft of Medical Workers," *New York Times,* October 19, 2004.

Peck, Fred, and Charles Rangel, "The Draft Debate," *American Legion,* June 2003.

Prah, Pamela M., "Draft Debates," *CQ Researcher,* August 19, 2005.

Quindlen, Anna, "Leaving on a Jet Plane: A Perfect Storm of Recent Historical Events Would Make a Draft More Divisive and Dangerous than Ever Before in the Nation's History," *Newsweek,* September 6, 2004.

Ricks, Thomas E., "Lukewarm on a Draft," *Washington Post,* November 1, 2004.

Robelen, Erik W., "Draft Talk Worries a Generation That Hasn't Seen One," *Education Week,* November 3, 2004.

Skoble, Aeon J., "Neither Slavery nor Involuntary Servitude," *Ideas on Liberty,* September 2003.

Swomley, John M., "Draft May Reopen So War-Making Can Expand," *Human Quest,* May/June 2004.

Thompson, Mark, and Michael Duffy, "Is the Army Stretched Too Thin?" *Time,* September 1, 2003.

Tucker, Cynthia, "Rich Pay Little for Freedom," *Atlanta Journal-Constitution,* May 30, 2004.

Tucker, Kyle, "Back (Door) Stabbed," *Political Affairs,* April 2005.

Williams, Walter, "Reinstating the Military Draft," *Conservative Chronicle,* May 12, 2004.

Wilson Quarterly, "A Return to the Draft? A Survey of Recent Articles," Autumn 2005.

Wooten, Evan M., "Banging on the Backdoor Draft: The Constitutional Validity of Stop-Loss in the Military," *William and Mary Law Review,* December 1, 2005.

Web Sites

FirstGov.gov: The U.S. Government's Official Web Portal (www.first gov.gov). A one-stop site that provides information about federal government agencies and provides Internet links to agencies and programs.

National Archives Online Veteran and Military Documents (www.archives.gov/veterans/research/online.html). Provides a variety of veteran records and military documents, including databases, online collections, and photographs.

Peace and Justice Support Network of Mennonite Church USA (peace.mennolink.org/youth). Produces information about recruitment and the draft, including information for potential conscientious objectors and resource links.

Index

enlistment. *See* All-Volunteer
Force; military draft; recruitment

Feith, Douglas, 57
Fick, Nathaniel, 36
Field, Herb, 11, 31
Freedom of Information Act,
49
Frontiero v. Richardson (1972),
72

Gates, Thomas J., 12
Gates Commission, 12–13,
15–16
GI Bill, 22
Glastris, Paul, 18
Graner, Charles, 57
Greeley, Andrew, 51

Habitat for Humanity, 62
Hagel, Chuck, 56
Harvey, Francis, 76
Herbert, Bob, 16
Heritage Foundation, 87
Hispanics, 82–85
Hollings, Fritz, 56
homeland security, 22
Hunter, Duncan, 76

Inouye, Arlene, 81
Iraq War, 49, 51
Abu Ghraib prison scandal
and, 57, 58

is being fought by working
and lower classes, 43–44,
62–63
limitations of U.S. military
power in, 24, 32, 35
volunteers serving in, 37
women in combat in, 77

Johnson, Shoshanna, 58

Kane, Tim, 87
Kerry, John, 54, 62
King, William R., 42
Korean War, 33, 51
Krohn, Charles A., 15–16

Leal, Rick, 82
Leonhardt, Nick, 54
lottery. *See* draft lottery
Lynch, Jessica, 58

Manning, Lory, 68
Marine Corps, 38–39
Mariscal, Jorge, 81
McHugh, John, 76
"Medal of Honor Tour,"
82–84
militarization, 59–60
military draft, 19, 33, 66
alienates youth, 51
benefits of, 34, 42, 61
educational aspects of, 22–23,
65
encourages war, 52

Picture Credits

Cover: © Leif Skoogfors/CORBIS
Maury Aaseng, 14, 33, 51, 70, 90
© Lynsey Addario/CORBIS, 34
AP/Wide World Photos, 32, 50, 53, 56, 63, 72, 79, 85
© Bettmann/CORBIS, 12, 19
Lance Cpl. Sheila M. Brooks, U.S. Marine Corps/Department of Defense, 67
Master Sgt. Jonathan F. Doti, U.S. Air Force/Department of Defense, 29
Airman 1st Class Nathan Doza, U.S. Air Force/Department of Defense, 64
Senior Airman Brian Ferguson, U.S. Air Force/Department of Defense, 39
Cpl. Brian M. Henner, U.S. Marine Corps/Department of Defense, 65
© Ed Kashi/CORBIS, 78
© Karen Kasmauski/CORBIS, 41
© David Leeson/*Dallas Morning News*/CORBIS SYGMA, 23
© Andrew Lichtenstein/CORBIS, 52
© Jerry McCrea/*Star Ledger*/CORBIS, 89
Petty Officer 1st Class Chad J. McNeeley, U.S. Navy/Department of Defense, 27
© Ed Murray/*Star Ledger*/CORBIS, 59
Senior Airman Desiree N. Palacios, U.S. Air Force/Department of Defense, 91
Senior Airman Kristin Ruleau, U.S. Air Force/ Department of Defense, 73
Petty Officer 1st Class Samuel W. Shavers, U.S. Navy/Department of Defense, 46
Petty Officer 2nd Class Bradley J. Sapp, U.S. Navy/Department of Defense, 77
© Leif Skoogfors/CORBIS, 13
© Swim Ink 2, LLC/CORBIS, 17
Mario Tama/Getty Images, 83
R.D. Ward/Department of Defense, 15
© Max Whittaker/CORBIS, 21, 43

About the Editor

George Milite is a writer and editor based in Philadelphia. He has written for numerous professional associations, including a number of leading resources in business, finance, and publishing. He is also an adjunct professor at The New School in New York and an instructor at Temple University. *Introducing Issues with Opposing Viewpoints: Military Draft* is his first title with Greenhaven Press.